A Reed Shaken With The Wind: A Love Story

Emily Faithfull

A REED SHAKEN

WITH

THE WIND:

A Love Story.

BY

EMILY FAITHFULL

"The variable as the shade,
  By the light quivering aspen made."

MARMION.

NEW YORK:
ADAMS, VICTOR & CO., PUBLISHERS,
98 WILLIAM STREET.

Entered according to Act of Congress, in the year 1873, by
ADAMS, VICTOR & CO.,
In the Office of the Librarian of Congress, at Washington.

Stereotyped at the
WOMEN'S PRINTING HOUSE,
No. 2 Mission Place, bet. Park and Worth Sts., one block East of Centre,
NEW YORK.

DEDICATION.

———•••———

TO MY FRIEND,

LAURA CURTIS BULLARD,

WHO RECEIVED ME ON MY FIRST ARRIVAL IN NEW YORK,

AND WHO,

TOGETHER WITH HER FAMILY AND MANY

OF HER

NOBLEST COUNTRYMEN AND WOMEN,

GAVE ME A PLEASANT EXPERIENCE

OF

GENUINE AMERICAN HOSPITALITY,

WHICH I SHALL EVER REMEMBER WITH AFFECTIONATE GRATITUDE.

"Whirling away
 Like leaf in the wind,
 Points of attachment
 Left daily behind,
 Fixed to no principle,
 Fast to no friend,
 Such our fidelity,
 Where is the end?"

HENRY ALFORD.

PREFACE.

THIS story is a simple analysis of one of the most dangerous phases of female character—a phase, alas! but too common in fashionable city life, on both sides of the Atlantic.

I have seen with my own eyes the curious combination of intellectual power and instability of purpose portrayed in Tiny Harewood; I have watched with an aching heart the shifting weaknesses and faint struggles for redemption described in these pages; I have known women, equally and honestly critical of their own faults, who, while capable of assuming the philosophical and moral tone, occasionally adopted by my heroine, and displaying a cool acumen and penetration of ethical questions, like her, persistently "the wrong pursued." Gifted with physical and mental attractions, although conscious of higher and nobler aspirations, some appeared unable to resist the temptation of exercising their perilous love of power, and accordingly drifted hopelessly away into the shallows and quicksands of life, extinguishing God's light in the soul by the myriad *conventional* crimes which are under the shelter of social, but not within the pale of moral, laws.

If the delineation of the chameleon nature of my English heroine, and the gradual crucifixion of the higher purpose beneath the destroying influence of a frivolous butterfly existence, enables one American reader to detect in time

> " That little rift within the lute
> Which by and by will make the music mute,
> And gently spreading, slowly silence all—"

the publication of this tale will not be in vain.

EMILY FAITHFULL.

BROOKLYN, N. Y., *May* 1, 1873.

·A REED
SHAKEN WITH THE WIND.

CHAPTER I.

" We stand on either side the sea,
  Stretch hands, blow kisses, sigh, and lean,
  I toward you, you toward me;
  But what hears either save the keen
  Gray sea between ? "

A. C. SWINBURNE.

    " Only I discern—
Infinite passion, and the pain
Of finite hearts that yearn."

ROBERT BROWNING.

ON a bright frosty day in December, not many
years ago, the Boulogne steamer started from the
pier at Folkestone, containing among its passengers an English family bound for a six-months'
residence in Rome.

The leave-takings were all over; friends who

had accompanied the "outward bound" to the
steamer had received the last distinguishable farewell nod; all who were left behind were already
tired of waving their hands, and had, one by one,
with a single exception, departed from the pier.

Wilfred Lane still lingered. His eyes had been
fixed upon a fair young face until it could no
longer be distinguished. He had watched the
slight figure of a girl who was looking earnestly at
the receding pier, as she leant over the side of
the boat, with her hand over her eyes, shading
her face from the sun. And now the steamer
itself seemed like a moving black mass on the
water.

At last the young man walked rapidly off the
pier, through the town, and, mounting the steep
hill beyond, turned his face once again towards
the sea.

There was the "Queen of the Isles," already
looking much smaller, and ploughing her way
across the Channel with cruel rapidity. Soon she
appeared like a thick black post, which Wilfred
watched until it grew fainter and fainter, and at
last he could discern nothing at all.

And yet he could not bear to leave the spot.
He felt, while he stayed there, away from every
other human being, and looked out upon the sea
in the direction where he had last seen the steamer,
that he was nearer to Tiny Harewood than he
should be when he went back again into the town.

Besides this, Wilfred Lane felt a curious choking kind of sensation in his throat, which he thought would get better if he remained in the open air alone.

CHAPTER II.

" Is human love the growth of human will ? "

LORD BYRON.

THE family on board the tidal boat in which
Wilfred Lane's interest was centred consisted of
his aunt and three cousins ; and the journey to
Rome was undertaken on account of his attachment to the youngest daughter—an attachment
which was warmly returned by the young lady
herself, but was unacceptable to the higher powers.

For many years Wilfred Lane had been in the
habit of frequenting Lady Harewood's house so
constantly that he had almost grown to look upon
it as his home. He was accustomed to do for her
and his cousins all those little offices which ladies
without near male relations are so glad to receive
from any man whom they regard in the light of a
"tame cat," or a cousin who will never step beyond certain limits, or claim any other reward for
his devotion than a kindly recognition of his ser-
vices. His aunt had hitherto received Wilfred's
attentions as her rightful due. Was he not the
only son of her husband's young and foolish sister

who, in spite of all her prudent counsels, persisted in refusing a wealthy unloved suitor in order to marry a poor country clergyman, who had not even the grace to live more than six months after Wilfred's birth, but left his widow as sole legacy a delicate little son, who must in future share with her the income which had barely sufficed for her own dress previous to this absurd love-match? And had not Lady Harewood done her utmost to supply a mother's place, ever since that same weak silly creature cried herself into an early grave? Did not Wilfred Lane owe his appointment in the War Office to interest exerted by her lamented husband?

In fact, Lady Harewood considered that she was only adding one more to the many favors already bestowed in allowing her nephew the free run of her house, permitting him to escort herself and her daughters to all the *fêtes* and balls of the season, to call up her carriage at the opera, and to undertake those many hundred little duties which force even the stoutest champions of woman's rights to acknowledge the supremacy of man.

Wilfred Lane on his part was nothing loth to accept the situation, although anything more opposed to his own character than that of his aunt's can scarcely be conceived. Lady Harewood was weak and frivolous, and the worldly maxims which she occasionally uttered for the benefit of his cousins, with the small amount of earnestness of which her nature was capable, were sometimes almost more than he could endure in silence. Placed by her marriage in a position above the rest of her family, which belonged to the trading class in the West of England, Lady Harewood appeared to live in constant dread of betraying it, and in order to disguise it she assumed what she believed to be the correct airs of a lady of fashion, and a sorry sort of figure she often made in consequence.

The three cousins were the silver lining to Wilfred's cloud, though there were moments when Charlotte showed tendencies to devote herself to the *beau monde*, like her mother; but they all inherited something of their father's marvellous intellect and genial disposition, and no house could fail to be agreeable which contained the bright and fascinating presence of these girls.

Men of all sorts clustered round them, and they made themselves agreeable to their own sex as well; still there were ladies who had hard words for the Miss Harewoods, and condemned them all three as " sad flirts." For, long before Tiny was eighteen, a well-known officer in the Life Guards had made her conspicuous by his public attentions, and gentle Belgravian voices were not slow to whisper that by the time Tiny was as old as her sisters she would have surpassed them both in the art of coquetry.

These insinuations, of course, never reached Wilfred's ear. He was regarded by the world

more as a brother than a cousin, and so indeed he
remained, until he learnt to distinguish between
the kindly pleasure with which he undertook to
ride or walk with Charlotte and Madeline, and the
different feelings he experienced when he found
Tiny's arm within his own. Then he felt no
longer a brother or mere cousin, for his pulse
quickened and his heart throbbed with a passion
unknown to such relationships. These were
dangerous times for Wilfred, but he did not shun
them, or think with any distinctness of that to
which they must ultimately lead.

As for Tiny, she was so full of life and spirits that
she seemed scarcely to notice any one save in a
passing way ; everything and everybody appeared
to give her pleasure for the moment, no one had
power to arrest her for longer. The admiration of
Captain Clutterbuck amused her and gratified her
vanity, but it certainly never touched her heart.
And so her nineteenth year passed away, and during the following winter the Harewoods went for a
month to some old friends who lived near Windsor.

It was Tiny's first visit to The Cedars, but she
soon became a great favorite with both host and
hostess, and when the time came for her mother's
departure, she had decided (for Tiny generally decided for herself) on accepting Mrs. Wroughton's
invitation to spend the rest of the winter at Windsor. Her motives were never much scrutinized
by her mother, who was in this instance ready to

agree to the plan proposed, and content to lose her child's companionship if by doing so she secured for Tiny the advantages which might accrue from visiting in "the best society in the neighborhood."

Though Lady Harewood had not the faintest notion how to promote them, good matches for her daughters were the end and aim of her existence. So she said good-by to Tiny with much hope and little regret, and retired with Charlotte and Madeline to Torquay, enjoying the satisfactory reflection that two daughters were much more conveniently chaperoned than three, and that Tiny's absence might even act beneficially for her sisters' interest as well as her own.

CHAPTER III.

"And barren corn makes bitter bread."

A. C. SWINBURNE.

"'Tis strange to think, if we could fling aside
The mask and mantle that love wears from pride,
How much would be, we now so little guess,
Deep in each heart's undreamed, unsought recess ;
The careless smile, like a gay banner borne,
The laugh of merriment, the lip of scorn,—
And, for a cloak, what is there that can be
So difficult to pierce as gayety ?
Too dazzling to be scanned, the haughty brow
Seems to hide something it would not avow ;
These are the bars, the curtain to the breast,
That shuns a scrutiny."

L. E. LANDON.

Now if the truth must be told, the society of
Mr. and Mrs. Wroughton did not constitute Tiny
Harewood's attraction to Windsor. She certainly
valued it as far as it went, nor was she by any
means insensible to the pleasures of a large country house, or unable to appreciate an establishment
containing among its most important members an
"exquisite French cook."

Tiny had a wonderful capacity for the enjoy-

ment of all material things, but her real induce-
ment to remain at The Cedars consisted in the
presence of a certain Captain Foy, who was staying with a maiden aunt in a cottage just on the
outskirts of the park.

Captain Philip Foy had found Mr. Wroughton's
society agreeable enough before the Harewoods'
arrival, and since then had never lost an opportunity of coming to the house. If he had intended
to tear himself away from his invalid aunt before
he made Tiny's acquaintance, he certainly never
contemplated such a sacrifice afterwards. He
certainly knew of places where he could have
better shooting, and many with more congenial
men companions, but it pleased him better to remain at Windsor, and to see what impression he
could make upon the warm, subtle, and half-per-
verse nature of Tiny Harewood.

Of course Captain Foy never meant " anything
serious." To begin with, he considered himself
too poor to marry, and when he did commit that
fatal act he intended it to be a stepping-stone to
his interests, which a marriage with a Miss Harewood was not likely, in his opinion, to afford.

Unfortunately poor Tiny mistook Captain Foy's
intentions. His brilliant social and intellectual
qualities so completely captivated her that she soon
fell violently in love with him, and believed he
was equally so with her.

Tiny Harewood was no ordinary girl, and perversity was one of her chief characteristics. Making sure that she was loved, and not feeling inclined to confess her own sentiments even to herself, she so teased, tormented, and worried the usually triumphant Captain Foy, that his love-making was often earnest enough, and once or twice he was nearly tempted to propose to her in spite of his firm resolution to keep within the limits which he had prescribed for himself.

One week followed another so rapidly, and the time passed so quickly while every day brought with it some mutual pleasure, that Easter arrived without a word from Tiny respecting her return home.

A summons, however, from her mother came at last, and though Captain Foy knew that Tiny's visit, like everything else in this world, had come to an end, he contented himself with being additionally tender, and even managed to kiss her in their parting interview in the shrubbery.

Wilfred, the useful cousin Wilfred, came down for Tiny and brought her back to London, which already gave symptoms of a gay and early season, and where she found her mother and sisters prepared for another campaign.

Tiny expected that before very long Captain Foy would contrive to call at Grosvenor Crescent. She knew it would be perfectly easy for him to find a hundred excuses for doing so, but that brave officer had no wish to put himself again in

temptation. He felt disposed to think that while
he had managed to amuse himself very pleasantly
during the winter, and enjoyed drawing out all
Tiny's exquisite coquetries, he had very mercifully
and wonderfully been kept within proper limits, in
not having positively made " a fool of himself" by
a definite offer of marriage.

Recognizing the nearness of the danger, however, he determined to avoid Miss Tiny Harewood
in future, and resolved to start another vehement
flirtation (for which, by the bye, he had a great
reputation) directly he got to London. He was
all the more inclined to do this when he found how
much he really missed Tiny's society, for he began
to fear that he had not come out as scathless from
this little episode as he at first fondly imagined.

All this time poor Tiny wondered why Captain
Foy never called. Sometimes she fancied he
would come on a particular afternoon, and then
she would resolutely stay at home. Once, when
she did this, she found her mother and sisters had
met him at the very afternoon reception to which
she refused to go, because she made up her mind
that the fastidious Captain Foy was sure not to go
to the Westbrooks, wherever else he might be.

At last, however, they met at Lady Howard's
dance, but Captain Foy appeared so engrossed
with Miss Peel that he only bowed when he first
saw Tiny. The partner she had been dancing
with had just brought her back to Lady Harewood,

who told her, as a pleasant piece of information which would greatly interest her, that Captain Foy was desperately in love with General Peel's daughter, and added, "it is everywhere reported that they are engaged."

Poor Tiny ! She felt as if all the brightness in her life had gone out, and that it would be impossible for her to know another happy moment. Her pride rebelled against the feeling that Captain Foy had only trifled with her affection, and her one comfort was in the thought that none of her home circle would ever know the deep and lasting impression which had been made upon her during her ever to be remembered visit to Windsor.

Turning to Wilfred, who came to claim her hand for the next waltz, Tiny was soon dancing with him, apparently the gayest and most light-hearted girl in the room ; and so well had she controlled her emotion, that when Captain Foy came up and spoke to her, she never even changed color, but answered him with such perfect friendliness and ease, that he was unable to flatter himself (which gave that gallant soldier a momentary pang of disappointment) that Tiny had come out less heartwhole than he had from a flirtation for which he would most certainly have been called to account, but for Mr. Wroughton's deafness, and Mrs. Wroughton's absence from the rides and walks during which it had taken place—to say nothing of the numerous casual meetings in the

shrubberies and park, of which they had both
been kept in complete ignorance.

But whatever appeared on the surface, poor
Tiny's heart ached enough below, and it was many
a long day before it ceased to pain her. At first
she took refuge in the most violent barefaced flirtations with the numerous suitors who were only
too eager to secure her notice, and she certainly
seemed more than likely to fulfil the amiable pro-
phecies of her lady friends.

It was in vain that Lady Harewood expostu-
lated, in her feeble fretful way, at these unseemly
proceedings, or that Tiny's sisters interfered.
Tiny was determined to flirt, and Tiny did flirt,
and once or twice she even passed the boundaries
of flirtation and inflicted on honest hearts the pain
she had herself experienced.

But Tiny's nature was really too good long to
remain satisfied with this kind of life. Gradually
her manner quieted down, and she seemed less inclined to take part in the different gayeties which
were going on, but entered, with a feeling more
akin to joy than anything she had felt since the
Windsor visit, into her cousin Wilfred's intellectual
pursuits and pleasures.

Wilfred Lane's delight was unbounded. Shut
out by his delicate health from the hardier games
and amusements of boys, books had always been
the world he really lived in, and when he saw with
daily increasing satisfaction that Tiny was being

drawn towards him, he gladly provided anything she cared to study, or read aloud to her while she worked or drew, much to the amused amazement of her sisters, who were, however, greatly relieved by seeing Tiny's whims taking a quieter and far less conspicuous turn.

Wilfred's greatest delight was in art, and though he never had produced anything himself, his appreciation and passionate love of painting had already gained him a considerable reputation as a critic, not only amongst his own immediate friends, but in the best literary circle. It therefore excited no surprise in Lady Harewood's mind when she saw Tiny studying Ruskin's "Modern Painters," preparatory to frequent expeditions with her cousin to the National Gallery—a place, be it remarked, strangely neglected by English people who crowd to the annual exhibitions of the Royal Academy, and profess to value good paintings, and sigh for Italy and the foreign places which contain them.

These were happy days for Wilfred, for he had an apt scholar, and his whole heart was in his work.

2

CHAPTER IV.

"The fountains mingle with the river
And the rivers with the ocean,
The winds of heaven mix forever
With a sweet emotion;
Nothing in the world is single;
All things by a law divine
In one another's being mingle—
Why not I with thine?"

PERCY BYSSHE SHELLEY.

TINY, perhaps, may not have felt absolutely happy, and she certainly was not *exaltée*, but she did feel she was living in a purer, higher atmosphere, and the worldliness of her mother and the frivolity of her sisters' pursuits began to grate upon her accordingly. She was beginning, too, to have a stronger feeling for her cousin than she had at first thought at all possible; and when she compared Wilfred's generous, unselfish character with others, and felt the influence of the high tone of mind which he brought to bear upon everything with which he came in contact, she could not help feeling his superiority to most of the men she ever knew—Captain Foy included.

One afternoon late in the summer Wilfred and

Tiny were sitting in a sheltered nook in the Belgrave Square gardens, having borrowed the key (a not unusual habit) from the Eliots. Wilfred had been reading aloud some of Mrs. Browning's "Sonnets from the Portuguese," and when he came to xliii. he paused, for he did not think he could trust himself to read it to Tiny. It was his favorite sonnet, and exactly expressed his feeling for his cousin.

Tiny, however, was imperative, especially when she saw that the page was marked, and a date written on it which her cousin refused to explain. At last he began—

"How do I love thee? Let me count the ways.
I love thee to the depth and breadth and height
My soul can reach, when feeling out of sight
For the ends of Being and ideal grace.
I love thee to the level of every day's
Most quiet need, by sun and candle light.
I love thee freely, as men strive for Right.
I love thee purely, as they turn from Praise.
I love thee with the passion put to use
In my old griefs, and with my childhood's faith.
I love thee with a love I seemed to lose
With my dead Saints—I love thee with the breath,
Smiles, tears, of all my life !—and, if God choose,
I shall but love thee better after Death."

As Wilfred read these lines in a voice of subdued passion, the truth which had lately been dawning upon Tiny's mind came to her in its full-

est force. She knew that she was *really* loved,
not with the same kind of love with which Captain
Foy had deceived her and amused himself, but
with a love which was Wilfred's very life, and
which would enable him to make any sacrifice of
his own feelings rather than wound or trouble her.
She was not excited by this knowledge, but she
was proud of having won Wilfred's affection ; and,
when he looked up, his cousin's eyes were fixed
upon his face, after that strange fashion of hers
which always made it difficult for him to control
himself. He lost all power to do so now :—the
book fell from his hand, his arm stole round her
waist, and their lips met for the first time.

.   . .   .

As Tiny walked back to Grosvenor Crescent
that afternoon she knew if she had not the full
measure of love to return, she had at least obtained
a heart which was hers completely.

But Tiny said nothing of this to her cousin ; she
kept to herself the unhappy episode with Captain
Foy, and allowed Wilfred Lane to suppose that his
love had been the first to awaken her own.

Now that Wilfred had been surprised into an
avowal to Tiny, he felt he must not keep it a
secret from her mother. Gathering up all his
courage he requested a few minutes' conversation
with his aunt after luncheon on the following Sunday ; but all the said courage seemed absolutely

oozing out at his fingers' ends as he followed Lady
Harewood upstairs, through the drawing-rooms
into her little boudoir. beyond.

Wilfred Lane knew that, with all her apparent
refinement, Lady Harewood could sometimes say
and do very rude things—so can every woman
whose school of manners has not been an honest
and true heart, but a smooth, false world.   He
expected his intimation to meet with considerable
opposition, but he was utterly unprepared for the
uncourteous treatment he received.   His relationship, as well as his deep love for Tiny, gave him
an unusually strong motive for keeping a firm
hand over himself, and for passing by personali-
ties which any other man would have felt justified
in resenting, even from a lady who might, one
day, become his mother-in-law.

Lady Harewood's anger seemed only equalled
by her amazement.   The idea of Wilfred's falling
in love with one of his cousins had never before
crossed her mind.   She would as soon have expected a proposal from him to herself.

It was some time before she could at all seize
the idea, and when she had done so, half an hour
did not suffice for the expression of her wrath and
disapprobation.

Accusing him of meanness and ingratitude, she
declared that, had his uncle lived, he would never
have dared to seek Tiny's love in such an underhand way, and wondered at his audacity in asking

her permission to take her daughter from " the lap of luxury " to such a home as he could offer. She proceeded to comment upon Wilfred's position and future prospects, and made allusions to his father which he felt quite unbearable, and resolved to answer when the torrent of words with which she assailed him showed symptoms of abatement.

He was about to do so, when Tiny made her appearance ; her mother's loud and angry tones reached her in the drawing-room, and excited her to such a degree that she felt she could not abide the issue of the conversation, but must go and take a share in it herself.

With a very pale face, and a quiet, determined manner, Tiny informed her mother that she came in to put a stop to any further difficulties, for she had resolved on marrying Wilfred, and Wilfred only; in token thereof she sat down by him, and, taking his hand in hers, seemed to defy her mother to offer any objection to such a conclusive and womanly argument.

Lady Harewood was much disconcerted by Tiny's entrance, but Wilfred felt considerably relieved. He hoped her daughter's presence would have some effect in inducing her to control herself. To tell the truth, he was positively alarmed at this exhibition of temper, as his aunt's delicate health and weak nerves were proverbial. Such a paroxysm of excitement might even produce a fit, he thought—a fainting, or hysterical scene, was

was the least evil with which he expected the afternoon to close.

It was one thing, however, for Lady Harewood to vent her indignation upon an unprotected man, whose position as her nephew made him singularly defenceless—to say nothing of the unusual amount of forbearance on which she knew she could count —but with Tiny it was quite another thing.

Having relieved herself by an outburst upon Wilfred, Lady Harewood was not going in her present exhausted condition to do battle with a young lady who was apt, under such circumstances, to get as excited as she did, and to return blow for blow. She therefore rose to her full height, and, with as much dignity as she could muster, rang the bell, and resumed her seat in silence.

When the old butler appeared, he was greatly surprised at receiving an immediate order for Lady Harewood's carriage. A Sunday afternoon drive was not among his lady's usual practices, though she did not scruple occasionally to require her carriage to take her to a quiet dinner-party. As Watson shut the door, Lady Harewood turned to Wilfred and requested him not to call before five o'clock on the following Sunday, by which he knew that he was expected to make himself scarce at once. Without any hesitation he said good-by to his aunt. While regretting that his wishes had met with such decided disapprobation, he hoped she would yet learn to look more favorably on his suit, and, with a pressure of Tiny's hand, which said more to her than a thousand words, he left the room.

Before Lady Harewood effected her escape Tiny heard the hall door close after Wilfred Lane. Then she and her mother had a sharp passage of arms, during which Tiny gave her to understand that she loved Wilfred, and was determined to marry him in spite of any opposition from the family.

CHAPTER V.

"Did'st thou but know the inly touch of love,
Thou would'st as soon go kindle fire with snow
As seek to quench the fire of love with words."

SHAKESPEARE.

LADY HAREWOOD was essentially a woman. She felt it impossible to get through the rest of the day without consulting somebody ; but, ready as she was to seek advice, she was seldom inclined to follow it.

In the present instance her thoughts turned to her husband's old friend Sir Anthony Claypole, and she resolved at once to ask his opinion on this unpleasant family difficulty. Wilfred's relationship had given him such access to Tiny that of course by this time they thoroughly understood each other, and probably had done so for weeks before the words were spoken which obliged them to take her into their confidence.

Although she determined not to countenance their "absurd and romantic attachment," Lady Harewood felt it by no means easy to forbid her husband's nephew the house.

On reaching Hyde Park Gardens, Lady Hare-

2*

wood found her friends surrounded by their usual number of Sunday-afternoon callers. She was prepared for this, and had left orders with the servants not to bring her carriage until half-past six o'clock.

This would give her ample opportunity for a quiet talk with Sir Anthony when the other visitors had dispersed. At present she must of course be content to join in the general conversation.

She thought that tiresome old Sir George Fullar never would leave off discoursing upon the epizootic, the number of horses he had lost, and the curious ways in which the disease made its appearance on his different farms ; but his departure was only the signal for Mrs. Redmarsh to commence a minute description of the fits her fourth baby had while cutting its teeth. Lady Ashworth being announced, the conversation took a political turn, until Mr. Hargrave drew every one's attention to himself by some clever remarks upon Lady Duff Gordon's " Letters from Egypt." He concluded by calling Lady Duff Gordon a most affected person, because the first sentence he saw on opening her book was, " I put my head out of the window this morning and delighted in the smell of the camels." Having lived a long time in the East, Mr. Hargrave proceeded to tell stories about camels, which tended to dispel any preconceived notions of the patience and docility of these animals, and certainly cast a serious reflection upon Lady Duff Gordon's olfactory nerves.

The drawing-rooms, however, were cleared at last, and then Lady Harewood told her friends her urgent reasons for seeking their advice.

It was so late when Lady Harewood returned home that there was hardly time to dress for dinner, which was more formal and uninteresting than usual.

Charlotte and Madeline had already guessed that their mother was ruffled by something of considerable importance, and Tiny felt but little inclined to enliven them by her ordinary sallies. It was a strange thing for Tiny to give way to depression, her spirits being in general equal to any emergency.

When the servants left the room after serving the dessert, Lady Harewood informed her daughters of the cause of Wilfred's non-appearance, and the sisters ascertained the correctness of their conclusions respecting Tiny's silence and red eyes.

Now, Charlotte had views of her own for Tiny. There was a certain young baronet, with £10,000 a year, who was desperately in love with her sister; and as Charlotte had discovered, after many exertions worthy of a better cause, that he would not transfer his affections to herself, she was extremely anxious to promote his wishes, and

induce Tiny to become Lady Fairfax, and mistress
of Downshire Hall, which she promised herself to
enliven by her own presence at seasons when the
county races and hunt balls made Buckingham-
shire more than usually attractive. She did not
feel in the least inclined to upset these pleasant
visions for the sake of Wilfred's proposal, and
accordingly came forward at once on her mother's
side, and expressed herself bound to consider
Tiny's real good rather than her present supposed
happiness ; and though Madeline was less inclined
to take an active part in the opposition to her
sister's wishes, especially when she saw her little
pleading face, she did not feel more disposed than
Charlotte to accept her cousin for a brother-in-
law.

Madeline also entertained strong opinions about
the marriages of cousins, and believed that their
children were always idiotic or blind, and she
honestly thought the good-natured Sir Guy Fairfax, with his comfortable rent-roll, a much more
suitable match. Wilfred was already like a
brother, and it certainly would be much better to
strengthen the position of the family by an
entirely new alliance.

But Tiny had been too long accustomed to have
her own way to yield to it on this occasion, so
she startled them all with the somewhat bold an-
nouncement that she " would rather never see her
mother or sisters again than be parted from Wil-

fred for a week." Retiring from the antagonistic
conclave she took refuge in her own room, from
whence she despatched a note to her cousin assur-
ing him of her affection, and saying that nothing
would induce her to change her mind, for her
whole happiness was centred in looking forward
to a life spent with him as his wife.

When Tiny left the room, Lady Harewood and
her elder daughters withdrew to the library, which
they generally inhabited on Sunday evenings.
She then told them of her visit to the Claypoles,
and how Sir Anthony had long ago suspected
Wilfred's attachment to Tiny, but had not noticed
it openly, fearing that to do so might bring about
the very result so deprecated by Lady Harewood.
Of course Sir Anthony felt Wilfred's prospects
made it natural for Tiny's mother to object to his
proposal; at the same time he observed that no
friend of the family could do otherwise than rejoice
at the change which had come over Tiny during
the last few weeks.

In common with many others, he had noticed
her previous flirtations, and had felt considerable
anxiety about her. He was often annoyed by remarks made at his club by men who did not spare
Tiny Harewood, but attributed her open and foolish transgression of the ordinary conventionalities
of society to an evil and wicked disposition which
would some day break loose altogether.

Although disinclined to place much faith in

Tiny's protestations of attachment to her cousin,
Sir Anthony Claypole feared that direct opposition would be the very way to fan the flame. He
did not believe in the · result of interference with
the young lady herself, but recommended Lady
Harewood to work through Wilfred, who would,
he thought, see the delicacy of his aunt's position, and the injury which would be inflicted on
Tiny if he persisted in holding her to an engagement of which her mother so thoroughly disapproved.

Before Lady Harewood left Hyde Park Gardens
she had (after judicious allusions to the lamented
Sir Henry's opinion of his friend's judgment, and
her own unprotected condition) induced Sir Anthony to promise that he would see the young
man, and place the matter before him from her
point of view.

Accordingly the post which brought Wilfred
Lane little Tiny's loving note, also conveyed to
him an invitation to dine at Hyde Park Gardens
on the following Tuesday; and, failing that, he
was requested to name an early day for seeing Sir
Anthony " on business of importance, undertaken
at Lady Harewood's request."

Wilfred had no particular engagement for that
evening, and impatiently waited for the time to
arrive when he should hear his aunt's decision.
He felt glad to think she had chosen Sir Anthony
Claypole for her mouthpiece, as he knew this

would give him a fair opportunity of stating his own case, and prevent a repetition of the scene which had so dismayed him on Sunday after-noon.

CHAPTER VI.

"Love took up the glass of Time, and turned it in his glowing
    hands ;
Every moment, lightly shaken, ran itself in golden sands.
Love took up the harp of Life, and smote on all the chords with
    might ;
Smote the chord of Self, that, trembling, pass'd in music out of
    sight."

ALFRED TENNYSON.

" He either fears his fate too much,
    Or his deserts are small,
Who dares not put it to the touch
    To win or lose it all."

MARQUIS OF MONTROSE.

As WILFRED LANE walked home that Tuesday
night across the park, he was not in an enviable
state of mind.

Sir Anthony Claypole had conscientiously fulfilled his promise to his friend, and had brought
before her nephew, in very decided language,
every obstacle he could think of to the proposed
marriage. He did not allow that he was at all
shaken by the young man's arguments, nor per-
mit Wilfred to see he had more than half won

over Lady Harewood's own advocate to his view of the case.

Wilfred Lane was clear upon one point only. In spite of all his shortcomings, and the errors into which, like most young men of his class, he had fallen, he felt himself not altogether unworthy of Tiny. He could offer her a pure strong love, and believed that, notwithstanding his position, a marriage with him would really be the best thing for her.

Wilfred was thoroughly in love, but his love did not altogether blind him to his cousin's failings. He knew she was terribly inclined to certain faults which might lead her into grave dangers, and that, with a most impulsive nature, she was just one of those girls who will be either very good or very bad—they know no medium—and are generally the latter, if their better and higher tastes are unsatisfied.

While Wilfred shrank from inducing Tiny to share with him a life of pecuniary difficulty and self-denial, he knew her well enough to feel that material ease was not over good for her, and that her character specially needed a home with a purer atmosphere than that of Grosvenor Crescent.

While capable of feeling a distaste for the general tone of London society, Tiny was yet liable to grow flippant in her own ideas and feelings, unless encouraged to live in the deeper part of life instead of on its mere surface. Nevertheless, she could scarcely become one of those anomalies, so often met with and yet so strange, which puzzle the moralist not by badness (which, alas! would be no anomaly at all), but by their power hanging on at such a very singular place in the scale of virtues and vices—a place which entirely ignores individuality; the result, probably, of living in and for society, and of never raising the thoughts to any high ideal, or letting them sink to the real passions of inner human life; but which, by following a meek dead idea of duty, maintain, in fact, the state which the word "respectability" best expresses.

Tiny Harewood was not one who would remain in a class of "respectables," which is ruled by a standard of right and wrong, made for the mass rather than the individual; so that Wilfred often feared, unless helped to strive after her own highest ideal, she would free herself altogether and become utterly reckless. He had watched her very closely of late, and though he had not the key to her wildness during the past year, it had caused him much anxiety and pain. When she turned from the frivolity and excitement of a fashionable life, which seemed to have such a bad effect upon her, he felt bound to give her all the help he could; and when that help had developed into love, he did not think himself justified in allowing a false spirit of honor to come between them.

It was true that, in comparison to Tiny, who inherited from her father an income of £800 a year, he was poor, and likely to remain so ; and it was anything but pleasant to a man of Wilfred Lane's sensitive nature to feel that his wife's income must go towards the mutual expenses of their home, instead of being devoted to the indulgence of her personal whims and fancies.

Then, too, he knew of Sir Guy Fairfax's attachment to Tiny, and could not shut his eyes to the advantages of such a connection to the family. When he thought over the many kindnesses he had received from his aunt, he shrank from the very idea of acting in an apparently ungrateful manner.

Essentially a proud man, Wilfred Lane felt almost tempted to relinquish his own happiness, and most probably would have done so but that he felt assured that Tiny had given him what she could never give to any other man—the first love of a very passionate nature. To resign this from a feeling of false honor, was to do her an injury for which no worldly advantage or position could ever atone, and Wilfred resolved never to do so.

Sir Anthony Claypole had not been unreasonable in his arguments, nor weakly violent like Lady Harewood, and Wilfred Lane spent the greater part of that night in battling with his own passionate love for his cousin, and in trying to see the matter from an unselfish point of view.

As morning dawned, he became somewhat calmer, and, lighting a cigar, determined upon following the course of action which at last suggested itself to his mind.

Lady Harewood had often talked of going to Rome—he would himself propose that she should do so this winter. Rome would be full of interests for Tiny—interests which could not fail to be good for her. If a marriage with him were really essential, a six-months' absence in such a place could do her no harm, and, in entirely different circumstances, she could follow more easily those pursuits and pleasures which seemed in keeping with her better nature. If, on the other hand, Tiny's love for him was less genuine than he believed it, such a separation would be a sure test, especially as he knew that, whether in Rome or London, the Harewoods would see plenty of society, and would certainly lose no opportunity of trying to wean his cousin's affections from himself.

The more Wilfred Lane thought of the self-sacrifice such a plan entailed the more he inclined to it, and though he knew Tiny must at first share with him the pain such a separation involved, he consoled himself with the reflection that her natural vivacity and light-heartedness, and the vivid pleasure which she took in every passing occurrence, would considerably diminish any suffering on her part, to say nothing of the intense delight a visit to Rome would be certain to afford a nature like hers.

Wilfred determined to see Sir Anthony Claypole before breakfast, for, like all lovers, his business appeared to him important enough to warrant an unusually early intrusion. After a couple of hours' sleep, refreshed by a bath and a cup of coffee, he soon crossed the Park, and, sending up his card, requested Sir Anthony to see him, as he had something of importance to say respecting their conversation on the previous night.

Sir Anthony Claypole thought Wilfred's proposal very reasonable—to say the truth, he was rather proud of the good result of his interference, and willingly undertook to see Lady Harewood during the day.

Wilfred wished his aunt to give him an early interview, but first to allow him to see Tiny alone.

" If," said he, " my aunt will agree to what is reasonable and fair, I will be patient; but I have determined not to sacrifice Tiny to pride on my part, or mere worldliness on hers."

True to his promise, Sir Anthony Claypole delivered the spirit of Wilfred Lane's message, but wisely suppressed the form of it. He advised Lady Harewood to adopt the plan suggested by her nephew, and agreed with her in thinking that such a separation would probably bring about the desired end. If-it failed to do so, Sir Anthony hoped Lady Harewood would no longer oppose the marriage. On this point, however, Tiny's mother was silent; she was content to accept Wilfred's sacrifice, and if that did not succeed, she would try some plan of her own.

When Tiny heard the winter was to be spent in Rome without Wilfred, she was furious. " Nothing would induce her to go," " she would sooner be a governess," " go on the stage," " sweep a crossing "—do anything, in short, rather than leave London, and it took a great many conversations (which, perhaps, Wilfred did not regret) to persuade her to yield.

At last, however, it was settled, and Tiny's unwilling consent given, on condition that she should be free to write to and hear from Wilfred during her absence, and that no opposition should be made to their marriage on her return.

To these conditions Sir Anthony gave his full consent; but then he was not her mother, or even her guardian. Still he was an important ally, and he undertook to do all he could to obtain Lady Harewood's concurrence. She, like a wise general, hastened the departure, and managed to effect it without having given any positive promise ; but Wilfred quieted Tiny by his belief that her mother tacitly accepted the conditions in following out the course suggested by himself.

The morning came for leaving London, and Wilfred Lane received a reluctant permission to accompany his aunt and cousins as far as Folkestone. Partly because Sir Anthony had good-naturedly interceded for him, but chiefly because Lady Harewood's courier was to join her in Paris, and, as she told Charlotte, "it was very inconvenient to have only a maid to help them with their bags and dressing-cases from the railway to the pier."

CHAPTER VII.

"With weary steps I loiter on,
  Tho' always under alter'd skies
  The purple from the distance dies,
My prospect and horizon gone.

    .   .   .   .

Oh yet we trust that somehow good
Will be the final goal of ill."

IN MEMORIAM.

WILFRED LANE was undergoing no ordinary
struggle. Looking across the English Channel
in the direction where he last saw the Boulogne
steamer, he realized in its fullest force the sacrifice
he had made ; and when he thought over the
possible results of this separation almost regretted
having insisted on Tiny's leaving him, and accused himself of allowing his pride—which resented his aunt's imputation of " taking advantage
of his position in the house to get Tiny completely
under his personal influence "—to conquer his
judgment.

Now the deed was really done he almost
repented of it altogether, and there were moments when he contemplated following the Harewoods by the next boat.

He knew Tiny's fine and ardent nature needed a better direction than it was likely to receive from her mother and sisters ; and when the balance is not struck between aspirations and the power which is able to realize them, a half-developed mind, no longer satisfied with common life, and to which some excitement is necessary, will seek its gratification in emotions and pleasures which are always dangerous and sometimes guilty.

Tiny Harewood still needed the constant presence of some wise loving counsellor to induce her to accept the " better part," and Wilfred could scarcely think with calmness over the dangers of repressed capabilities and unsatisfied desires which, for want of being helped towards the good and true, too often fix themselves on the bad and false. An incomplete development is a dangerous stage—a higher horizon is discerned, but there is not sufficient strength to reach it.

Wilfred felt but little comfort at this moment in remembering that in making his decision he had really tried to choose what appeared the best for Tiny, and that her mother considered he had succeeded in doing so. After all Tiny was bound to be subject to her mother, and an open defiance of a parent's wishes was not what Wilfred would lightly encourage. A compromise at present was all that could be thought of, and that entailed this Roman visit.

3

Another thought also crossed his mind. If Tiny could not stand the test of a six-months' separation, was her love really deep enough to enable her to share a whole life with him, without regretting her choice when the charms of novelty and satisfied affection had given place to the difficulties which find their way into the happiest home? If this were so, would he not be undertaking more responsibility than he ought—more indeed than he was capable of?

Walking slowly down the hill, Wilfred Lane went to the restaurant of the Pavilion Hotel, where he lunched, before returning to the station. He had arranged to stop on the line to see an old friend, now a country parson with a wife and one or two olive branches. He left Folkestone by the tidal express, and when the train stopped at the Red Hill Station, the Rev. Henry Frampton was waiting for him in a very unorthodox dog-cart, with the pleasing intelligence that Mrs. Frampton had presented him with a fine little son early that morning.

So Lane had just come in time to enjoy a cosey bachelor dinner with Harry Frampton, and it must be confessed that the young Rector rejoiced in the idea of a long talk over old school-days with his class-mate, accompanied by an unlimited supply of pipes and whiskey, for which he would not be called to account by his wife.

And a good talk they had far into the night, although Wilfred avoided the subject nearest his heart, and Frampton's conversation was somewhat altered—perhaps for the better, since his college days—in spite of the nursery anecdotes, for example, which now formed a new and not unimportant item, but among these he told a story for which Lane was willing to forgive the rest.   The birth of the new brother had duly been announced to little Katie Frampton by her father, and not very many minutes after he left the nursery, the child was found on her knees praying that "another little baby might be sent directly." It was also strange, when talking over the world and its ways and settling that it was better if possible to live your own life *out* of it, to hear Harry Frampton assert an entire belief in his wife's opinion that "the queerness of the age was to be attributed to the introduction of the new feeding-bottles, which enabled babies six months old to feed themselves."

The next morning Wilfred returned to London by an early train.   He had little opportunity, however, to indulge his own reflections, thanks to the pertinacy of a fellow-traveller—a man with a shining countenance and a double chin—who persisted in making, with a self-satisfied air, the most commonplace observations upon the appropriateness and use of all things in nature. When this man remarked that "trees were green because green is good for the eyes," Wilfred could no longer refrain from quoting Heine's answer on a similar occasion; and, assenting to his companion's proposition, he added that "cattle were made because beef soup strengthened man, that jackasses were created to serve as comparisons, and that man existed that he might eat beef soup and realize that he was no jackass;" a quotation which freed him from further interruption, and doubtless gave the possessor of appropriate ideas sufficient food for thought during the rest of the journey.

By a few minutes after ten o'clock Wilfred Lane was at his place in the War Office; everything belonging to his outward life was going on in the same way; people were coming in and out, the usual amount of business was being transacted, London was as full as ever, but yet to him life seemed going on with its heart out.

He got through his work, and after dinner strolled into the Haymarket Theatre. Feeling disinclined to read and incapable of writing, he thought while his pain was fresh it was wiser to distract his mind from his own griefs by the representation of unreal ones, than to brood over the events of the last two days and their probable effects.

CHAPTER VIII.

" WILHELM VON HUMBOLDT says, 'Old letters lose their vitality.'

"Not true. It is because they retain their vitality that it is so dangerous to keep some letters—so wicked to burn others."

MRS. JAMESON.

FIVE days after Wilfred's return from Folkestone he found a foreign letter on his breakfast-table. He opened it and read as follows :

" MARSEILLES, Wednesday.

" I watched till I saw only one person left on the pier. Was that you? It isn't the pain of parting which is the worst to bear, darling Wil, it is finding out more and more the loneliness of life without the one whom I love best, and love most in the every-day commonplace hours of life, no, not commonplace when my own Wil is near, to sweeten and purify every moment. This is eating the very hardest bread and cheese of life after the sweetest fruits of true love.

" I slept a little in the train to Paris, and woke realizing more than I had hitherto done that the part of myself I most cared to call my own was

every moment being left farther behind. After
our night's rest in Paris, mamma determined on
coming straight through to Marseilles, and we certainly managed the journey with as little fatigue as
it is possible to imagine. I slept nearly all the
night, which helped to make the sixteen hours
pass more quickly ; we got here at half-past twelve
in the morning, and, to make up for any rest we
might have lost, we had fourteen hours' real sleep
last night.

" I enjoyed looking out of the windows as the
sun rose—such a blue sky and bright sun. The
country is very pretty between Lyons and Marseilles. You see the Alps in the distance covered
with snow, and the railway runs for some time
along the Rhône, and the pink light made it all so
pretty.

" Mamma retired early, and Charlotte said such
very aggravating things about you that it ended
in our having a regular quarrel, after which we all
went to bed. Mamma telling me through the
door that I talked so loud it made her head ache,
which I thought very unfair, having said one word
to Charlotte's twenty, and about the same propor-
tion in sound. After this little excitement I slept
for thirteen hours, and then thought I would have
some breakfast in bed to recover my equilibrium.
Madeline came to me afterwards and read ' Co-
rinne ' while I dressed, and then we all trotted out
and went to the top of a hill, from which we had a

most splendid view of the town and hill behind, and the sea and bay of Marseilles in front. It is really a very handsome town, and I enjoyed my walk as much as I could without my own arm to lean on.

" I suppose you are back at your work. I hope you will repent of your cruelty in sending your unhappy little Tiny away. If you had been me, and I you, I am sure I should never have had the heart to do it, and I don't believe you love me a bit. But you will find it quite useless. Being away from you only shows me how much I love you, and I will never give you up unless you find some one whom you love too well to send away to Rome for a whole winter; but you will never find any one who will love you half as much as your Tiny.

" P.S.—If I don't find a long letter waiting for me in Rome, I shall never forgive you. I hope we shall have a good passage, the sea seems very calm, and there is no wind at present."

Wilfred Lane was not the man to make a half sacrifice. If Tiny could be induced to regard him simply as a cousin, he determined never to hold her to the repeated promises she had made since that day in the Belgrave Square gardens, when he betrayed his love. In suggesting this six-months' absence, he felt that her mother and sisters would have every opportunity to influence her ultimate decision, and that Tiny herself, after the first pain

of parting, would be better able to judge of the
strength of her attachment when quite out of the
reach of his personal influence, which was, he knew,
of a very remarkable kind.

Wilfred was generally able, without any effort on
his part, to establish a sympathy between himself
and people with whom he came in contact, even if
they were previously prejudiced against him.

Without being handsome his face was decidedly
attractive, with a mass of rich brown hair brushed
back from a full, earnest brow.   No one with anything artistic in their composition could refrain
from watching the variety of expressions which
passed over his face in the course of an hour, and
women, especially, felt the power of his dark expressive eyes, through which a singularly determined will made itself understood, in spite of a
yielding manner.   Yet to some people Wilfred's
chief fascination was in a voice, which was very
remarkable for its varied intonations.   Of a medium pitch, soft, yet exceedingly clear, and capable
of wonderful modulation, there was an irresistible
charm in his speaking voice, which even men considered " soothing," and which gave him an unusually strong and often entirely unsought-for dominion over the other sex.

Recognizing the power of this personal influence
to a certain degree, though far from realizing its
full effects, Wilfred thought that while he could
never of his own free will have imposed such a test

upon Tiny Harewood, he did not feel it an undesirable one, when he remembered her peculiarly impulsive, impressionable nature.

Of course he knew that Tiny would be unhappy at first, but unless he was really essential to her life he questioned whether she would long remain so, in a place which would be full of interest. He therefore determined on leaving her while in Rome as free as possible. If by assuming a quiet cousinly tone he could induce her to return to their old relationship, he resolved to control himself and to conquer his own deep love.

Nothing short of a whole-hearted effort on his part would satisfy his conscience, or justify the decided opposition he intended to offer his aunt, should Tiny remain true to the feeling she now entertained for him, and Lady Harewood still refuse her consent to their marriage.

Accordingly the letter which greeted Tiny on her arrival in Rome quite astonished her. Instead of any regrets over her departure, or groans over his own loneliness, Wilfred simply acknowledged her letter from Marseilles. After saying that he had no London news or gossip of any description to send, he added : " If you care to please me you will make yourself as happy as you can in Rome, and you ought not to be miserable in such a place. If you will throw yourself into the interests by which you are surrounded, the time will pass all the quicker, and you will not have to regret lost

opportunities—opportunities which will scarcely
come again if you marry me.

"Do not think me cold, for it costs me more
than I dare tell you to urge what I think due to
you as well as to your mother. Remember, if *at
any time* during this absence you can persuade
' yourself that your whole happiness is not bound
up in our mutual love, if you can possibly free
yourself from the feeling which at present binds
you to me, I implore you to do so.

"Life, with me, will be very full of material
difficulties, and I could not bear to think I had put
out the sweet sunshine of *your* life. Do not come
back to me unless you feel certain that your love
for me is so strong that you could not be happy
without me. I shall not allude to this again, but
remember that, if now,—a little later,—or even
during your last week in Rome, you are able to
resume your old cousinly footing with me, I will
never blame you for it, but have myself invited
you to do so.

"But if, Tiny, you feel your happiness completely linked with mine, the devotion of my entire
life shall be yours, and I shall never cease to thank
God for a blessing so great, that every outward trial
will be lost sight of in the sense of that deep joy."

When Tiny received this letter she almost felt
inclined to be angry with Wilfred. It was absurd
to suppose she should change. She loved her
cousin, and she meant to marry him, although she

knew she had once had a deeper feeling for another. When she first realized that Captain Foy had only trifled with her affection, she never intended to marry anybody, and began to take an interest in Wilfred without ever dreaming of caring for him in the same passionate way. Gradually his love, from soothing her, became essential, and her real sympathy with his tastes and pursuits gave her a greater sense of rest and quiet than she had yet experienced.

Even those who had put the worst construction on Tiny's flirtations in the first days of her bitter disappointment were less conscious than she was herself of the innate wildness from which they sprang—a wildness which was not very far from developing into wickedness. Once or twice she became so thoroughly reckless that even she had been positively frightened.

In her calmer moments she longed for an influence strong enough to arrest her ; her own principles were too unformed, and her impulses far too strong, ever to be controlled by the mere worldly maxims which were the standard of her home, and sufficed for less unmanageable natures. In spite of the unusually strong physical temperament which her early education, and the kind of life she had led, developed, Tiny knew of another side which Wilfred had called into fuller existence. To cultivate this higher part of her character was not only to satisfy her intense craving after what

was really noble and pure, but she believed it to
be the only safeguard against temptations to which
she was strongly inclined. Too weak to trust herself, or to stand alone, she looked upon Wilfred's
love as a special Providence, from which, at first,
she dared not turn, and to which she finally gladly
yielded herself, believing that her feeling for Captain Foy was the first passionate love which is so
seldom realized in this world, and that her affection for Wilfred was enough to satisfy her, especially as he had already elicited a. much stronger
response than she ever supposed she could give
any one else. That she had won the affections of
a man whose character she so intensely respected,
gratified her—the opposition she encountered from
her family aroused the perversity of her disposition, and her enforced separation kindled her imagination, until she forgot her past feeling in the
longing for the daily and hourly sympathy and
love she received from Wilfred, the want of which
now made such a void that her life seemed worth-
less unless shared with him.

It was true that her love for Captain Foy had
made a lasting impression, but it was also true that
at the present moment she was really in love with
Wilfred Lane. Tiny Harewood was not one of
those who love once and forever ; she loved with
her whole nature for the time being, but it was a
nature capable of " change upon change "—a nature often combined with vivid imagination and

intellectual power, but rarely united with the depth and earnestness possessed by Tiny. Her character was singularly intricate, and Wilfred, fascinated by her childish grace and apparent frankness, believed in the ultimate development of the beautiful qualities which existed in rare profusion among the baser elements of this peculiarly gifted being. The finer the nature the more flaws will it show through the clearness of it. The best things are not often seen in their best form. The wild grass grows well and strongly one year with another, but the wheat is, by reason of its greater nobleness, liable to the more bitter blight.

Wilfred often remembered a saying of Mrs. Jameson's, as he thought over Tiny's character : " Good principles derive life and strength and warmth from high and good passions ; they do not give life, they only bind up life into a consistent whole. We are not to take for granted that passions can only be bad, and are to be ignored and repressed altogether—an old mischievous, monkish doctrine."

The great thing was, not to inculcate principle, but to train Tiny's feeling, and he could not prefer a more perfect character in its narrower requirements to what appeared so much higher and nobler, though mingled with many faults. He believed that all Tiny really wanted was wise guidance, and that the past circumstances of her life had exposed her to many dangers, especially to the pursuit of false pleasure. He had watched her abandon her early instinctive delight in true pleasures, sacrificing her natural and pure enjoyment to her pride, and he thought she had already discovered that these were the bitterest apples of Sodom on which she could feed.

It was very strange, but equally true, that Wilfred Lane, like many other men before him, lived day by day by the side of her he loved best, and never guessed the secret influence which acted in such a powerful way on Tiny's soul, nor the hidden life carried on within the folds of her outward existence. Had he done so—had he but known the feelings with which Tiny still regarded Captain Foy, and had glided into her present relation with him, he might have acted differently; and, instead of giving her the choice of returning to him or otherwise, he would have understood her divided heart better than she did herself, and would have shown a resolute regard for their future interests, in spite of present suffering. He might not have blamed her, for it is the propensity of an ardent nature to love and trust notwithstanding disappointment, just as a flower throws out fresh buds again and again, only to be nipped by a killing frost; but he would never have treasured up the belief that he had been the one to excite in Tiny's heart the deepest feeling of her life, and that her nature, once roused to a sense of his love, and giving such a full and free response to it, could know no change.

CHAPTER IX.

PERHAPS few women would have appreciated Wilfred Lane's letter if addressed to themselves. They prefer to hear from their lovers how impossible life is without them, and that, in spite of parents or guardians, they will carry them off to the other end of the world rather than give up the being in whose existence their own is merged, and that, if tempted by any one to prove unfaithful, deeds of violence will ensue, for no revenge will be too great for them to take upon any one who supplants them in the heart of the " only woman

who has ever had sufficient power to kindle in
their own the undying flame of a deep and life-
long attachment,"—and so forth !

Anyhow, Lady Harewood was probably the
only person in this instance who would have really
liked Wilfred's letter, had she seen it, and even
she would have thought it much more sensible if
the last sentence had been omitted.

It certainly did not please Tiny in her present
state of mind, and she resolved to express her
sentiments very clearly, and did so in the following manner :

"Rome.

"You absurd, aggravating Wil, I don't know
if I ought not to be very angry with you. I shall
not have any consideration for your feelings, I
shall only consider my own, and come back to you
and claim my right to torment you for the rest of
your natural existence. I don't care what objections you like to raise ; never was your love so
necessary as it feels now, though, I daresay, it is
very improper and unlady-like of me to tell you
so. I think it is very unmanly of you to be afraid
of mamma and compel me to fight our battles or
allow you gracefully to retire from the field. No,
Mr. Wilfred Lane, I don't intend to let you off so
easily. You often correct me for little wee faults
(and by the way you have no business to see any
in me, at all), and you allow yourself the most unlimited amount of the worst sin a man, woman, or

child can indulge in—PRIDE. Because I am
obliged to confess to you that I am very miserable
without you, and don't continually brandish over
you the fear of losing me, you take up a tone
which I think most unbecoming. However, I
will soon do something to bring you on your knees
again—the right position for both of us. I am
glad you say you shall ' not allude to this again ; '
I make you a profound curtsey, sir, and beg you
to waste no more time in writing ridiculous letters.
I suppose you wrote the last because you had
nothing else to do, or wanted to cultivate a new
style ! Anyhow, you only wrote it because you
knew your self-denial would be received with appropriate indignation and scorn. But, as you are
always quoting Sir Peter Teazle's naughty expression about sentiment, I shall leave this subject
and tell you of our journey.

" We had an awful passage. It was quite calm
when we started ; but the wind rose very soon,
and we tossed about fearfully, and towards morning had to put back into the harbor of Toulon,
where we remained a day and a night. Most of
the passengers were very ill. I stayed on deck,
watching such a beautiful moonlight on the water,
and the mountains, which are all round the harbor,
reminding one of Gibraltar—quite a land-locked
harbor, and full of French men-of-war. One of
them sent up rockets and burnt blue lights, apparently for my edification.

" How you would have enjoyed seeing the rip-
pling water lit up by the moon and the lights from
the ships. Such a pretty color it is, a tender deep
blue, always shifting into golden ripples, and then
the dark hills with a bright line of lights and their
reflections—some creeping up the sides and struggling quite high up the hills, and, beyond all this,
the gray mountains rising against the clear bright
sky.

" I looked, too, at the pretty setting of the stars
—you gave me that idea—but then what a different sky they are set in here !

" The worst part of our passage was between
Toulon and Villafranca. We spent a miserable
day—trying to run along the coast, then attempting the open sea, tossing and dancing about,
making no way at all. But at last it came to an
end, and here we are in Rome.

" This is *such* a place ! The climate is delicious, and everything one sees surpasses one's
expectations. Not exactly that anything we have
seen is beautiful, but everything is so interesting
and picturesque, and has a character of its own,
and a completeness of association which makes one
enjoy it much more than simply beautiful buildings. Not that I feel inclined to enjoy anything ;
when I think of you in that grimy, foggy, old
London, I feel as if I were cut in two, and that
the best half of me were there, not here.

" The charm of this place I cannot describe,

but you of all people would appreciate it. We have a lovely garden to this hotel, which we can get to by a terrace leading from a passage outside our rooms. It is full of fountains and flowers, lovely shrubs, and terraces, where you could smoke and enjoy yourself in the sun by day, and in the moon by night, and I could come down to my own strong Wil, when I felt I needed to be calmed and soothed.

" I don't lead my own life a bit with the others; of course it is no fault of theirs, but one's own weakness. So it is. I am pulled along with the stream, theoretically wishing to go one way, but practically having all one's time, mind, and nerves used up in the family life.

" Charlotte is just singing Schubert's ' Parting of Hector from his Wife.' I daresay you don't know it, but you ought to. It is, perhaps, a slightly classical parting, but it is a good downright sort of one, strong, hopeful, and wildly intoxicated with love.

" Wilfred ! if you were ever sure of anything in this world, you may be sure of the good effect of your love upon me. When I think of what you have saved me from, I can't help thanking God for it. You have done what no saint, or angel, or anything less human, could have effected, and given reality and form to what were only vague, occasional sentiments—dreamy, unreal sort of impulses.

"I go on with my readings of the two Brownings and Ruskin. I think Ruskin is very like the Bible—the Bible made comprehensible, just what is divine taken out, but much of the beauty and purity left in.

"Yesterday I saw a perfect picture—Raphael's Fiddler. Such a face, Wil, rather the type of his own, but not so fair, and instead of the dreamy, loving expression of the Louvre portrait, a perfect load of Art—sensitive, passionate Art—the whole countenance sad, not wholly beautiful—as no artist's face ought ever to be made. *To do* and *to be* are quite incompatible, don't you think so? I think, somehow, artists ought not to be beautiful, or their personal influence detracts from the influence of their Art, for after all there is nothing like people, and it is not fair to oppose them to any Art whatever. But Raphael's Fiddler is so steeped in his Art, that one hardly thinks whether it is a man, a boy, or a woman. He has no individuality but his Art. I have been thinking of him ever since, and can't get him out of my head, with his dark face, and matted hair, cut straight along the forehead, surmounted by a little black cap. The fur tippet he wears is something quite beyond admiration—a most delightful mixture of yellow, brown, and gray—over a sad green dress, and the fiddle itself a red brown. Some dark blue flowers with rich green leaves are in his hand, and all besides is well kept in the shade. I have gone quite wild over this picture, and can think of nothing else.

" I send you a few of what we agreed together were favorite flowers of ours—do you remember ? I got them in the Ludovici Gardens. Such a view we had from the top of the villa !

" A stormy day, raining a little—and all the ilexes and cypresses ink-black in the foreground, and, beyond, a burning sheet of gold on the Campagna, and the piles of mountains all mixed up in the clouds ; some bright peaks of snow with bronze light, the stormy, violent light that gives snow such a wonderful color, reminding one at the same time of metal and of the softest, mellowest swan's plumage. Then, the next mountain the fullest lapis blue, and far off in the sunshine Soracte piled up all alone, quite light cobalt in a sky of the fairest blue (like an old Francia's sky), as if it knew nothing whatever about what was going on in the dismal parts of the heavens. The only thing that was not ink-black in the foreground was the Tiber, and Heaven only knows where it got its flaming brightness as it twisted under the black clouds on its winding way. Yes, Rome is a wonderful place when you see all that (and a thousand things besides) up at the top of a tower, and at the bottom such statues as the Mars in repose, the Juno's head, and several others which are beyond description beautiful.

" One of the best pictures I have seen was at a

concert the other night. A quartett of Mozart,
played by Madlle. Julie, two violins, and a violon-
cello. Madlle. Julie's face—as I saw its profile—
all full of earnest quiet music, with the load in the
eyebrows which in musicians seems to me to express all the pain of Art—the spirit much too
strong for utterance, a bewilderment of the brain
in the higher regions—a quiet, sensitive mouth, a
yellow skin, the same all over (no artist ever had
a good complexion, I'm sure) and black unnotice-
able hair. If you have ever seen Rubenstein you
will understand what I mean by the load in the
eyebrows. Then came the violins and violon-
cellos, and interesting clever musician-faces playing them, half hid by the pretty curves of their
instruments and the stands for their music, all
their black coats, and Madlle. Julie's simple black
dress without a white collar even, all more than
half hid, but coming so well and seriously against
the wall behind. The wall of the theatre is
painted with a full, soft drapery, with little gold
touchings here and there—all much hurt by time,
and therefore the better for the picture. It was
altogether perfect, as the colors of the instruments
—yellow, red, and brown mingled—and the sallow
faces of the players looked perfectly delightful
against the subdued green background. But of
course the music in the faces (particularly in
Madlle. Julie's) made the picture. It reminded
me so of George Sand's ' Consuelo,' which is full

of artistic scenes; Haydn and Co.'s little musical meetings in the old musical atmosphere of the old times—all old—nothing of the nineteenth century about them.

" But now I have well dosed you with my prosings, I shall only add that what Rome would be to me under favorable circumstances I cannot imagine. You see if I am only to write occasionally I mean to send you letters you cannot read all in a minute, but which will compel you to think for at least one half hour after you receive them of the unfortunate

" little exile,

" TINY HAREWOOD."

CHAPTER X.

" And this woman says, ' My days were sunless, and my nights were
    moonless,
Parched the pleasant April herbage, and the lark's heart outbreak
    tuneless,
If you loved me not ! '   And I who (ah, for words of flame !) adore
    her !
Who am mad to lay my spirit prostrate palpably before her—"
                                        ROBERT BROWNING.

WILFRED was delighted with this letter ; not
only for its freshness and keenness of appreciation,
but for the loving steadfastness it expressed for
him. He declared to himself that Tiny was like
a pemmican, or jelly, or anything which contains
a lot of strength, but is little in size ; and it seemed
to him that the good qualities of six or eight ordinary good women were boiled down to make her
what she was, and that was why she was not bigger !

Had the letter been answered that day, Wilfred
felt he must have given vent to all the loving feelings of his heart, and therefore he put it in his
pocket and resolved on allowing a week to pass
before he trusted himself to write to " his little
sunshine," as he often called Tiny. But he only
found each day made him more hungry, and it

sometimes seemed impossible to repress his passionate love. Nothing but the conviction that this complete sacrifice best proved his true affection, enabled him to resist the desire of telling her how entirely his life was bound up in hers. Sometimes the craving was so strong that he was forced to yield, but the letters written in these moments were never posted.

This was the answer sent to Tiny.

" MY DEAR LITTLE SPRITE :

" If I am afraid of your mother, I am not going to be terrified by you, and shall therefore continue to give you cause to scold me to your heart's content—for the present—waiting, however, a fitting opportunity to punish you for your evil deeds. If that day ever comes you will cry aloud and in vain for mercy.

" Instead of all these reproaches your letters ought to be written in a strain of continual thanksgiving for the pleasures I have been benevolent enough to procure you this winter.

" Think of the lovely climate with which you are enraptured, and then fancy my mistaking a lamp-post for a man on my way to the office this morning—a wrong conclusion, which brought speedy retribution in the shape of a sudden collision of a remarkably severe nature.

" See what a wise old cousin you have ; wise as well as benevolent !

4

" I knew Rome would enchant and fill you with happy, beautiful thoughts ; but I hardly ever expected you would enable me to share them so completely by sending such gloriously vivid descriptions of all you see and hear.   I feel as if I had seen Raphael's Fiddler now, but I don't quite see that ' *to be* and *to do* are incompatible,' even in relation to outward beauty and artistic work, and I am sure, my dear little coz, it isn't so with regard to other things, inasmuch as the *being* must come before the *doing*.   Eh ?

" But you must be content with shabby answers ; for *I* have nothing beautiful to write about. I can only tell you of the books I am reading, one of which you would enjoy immensely.   A certain Dr. Carl Vogt, who has written on ' Man and his Place in Creation,' believes that, as animals have brains, they have intellects ; and his book abounds in stories of religious dogs, just cats, bears and apes, with notions of dignity and decorum.   In the way of novels, I have been skimming ' Emily Chester,' which works out the theory that God gives to every creature the exact discipline which best tends to promote its final development. With those to whom happiness is the one possible means of expansion—their characters requiring moral sunshine, just as some flowers need the physical—it almost seems as if ' an angel had charge concerning them, lest they dashed their foot against a stone ; ' while to others, pain and suffering seem to be their positive nutriment—fire their native element.

"How glad I am you are going on with your readings from Ruskin and the Brownings. To me there is an intense life in 'Aurora Leigh;' it is certainly a great poem, notwithstanding a want of finish which suggests masculine rudeness of power, rather than feminine delicacy of touch.

"I. saw a very good thing in a criticism on Robert Browning the other day. The writer, in speaking of his obscurity, says, by way of example, that one of his poems contains only two intelligible lines, and that these two are not true. The first line is

> ' Who will, may hear Sordello's story told.'

with which the poem commences, and the other is the one with which it concludes,

> ' Who would, has heard Sordello's story told,'

I believe this is the poem of which Browning's father exclaimed, ' I spent the whole morning over it, but I could only make out that there was a woman in it.'

"And now I must leave off writing, but I shall not leave off longing for your next letter until I have received it. Give my love to Charlotte and Madeline, and an appropriate message to your mother.

"Ever yours,   "W. L."

CHAPTER XI.

" Majesty,
Power, glory, strength, and beauty, all are aisled
In this eternal ark of worship undefiled."

LORD BYRON.

WILFRED had not very long to wait, although it
appeared long enough to him, before his eyes
were gladdened by the sight which had now become so precious to him, of a yellow envelope,
bearing the Roman postmark.

Breaking the seal, he read:

"You cruel Wilfred, to mount such a pedestal
when I have become dependent upon your kind
words. I feel every thought of the future so
bound up in your strengthening love that I long
for its expression even on a miserable sheet of
paper. And you must give it, for I am so lonely,
and should feel quite another person if I could
only have a hopeful loving letter from you. Oh,
Wil, it is such an age since that horrid steamer
took me away from the figure on the Folkestone
pier. One's cheerfulness is beginning to be a
melancholy failure, such a skull-like grin! I had

a great fright too, yesterday. I looked down at my arm and saw I had lost your dear locket off my bracelet. Fancy my concern! I hunted everywhere, and so did every one else, till at last I went to bed in despair, hardly able to sleep for the thought of it. In the morning Smith brought it in, saying she had found it in the passage the night before.

"The other day two of the Leighs called and asked us to go with them to see the fox hounds meet, so I went with Madeline. It was a splendid morning, and we had such a pretty drive, the views of the mountains with their tops all covered with snow, and quite pink in the morning light, were lovely. Lady Emily Cavendish was first and foremost, with red hair, red tie, gold spangled net, bright blue habit, and on a gray horse. She looks well on horseback, however, rides capitally, and won the fox's brush on Monday. One of the best riders and most constant lady hunters in Rome is the bright vivacious Harriet Hosmer, the famous American sculptress.

"And now I must tell you about our Christmas Eve.

"We went with the Somervilles and Dunmores, in three carriages, through the deserted streets; there are only patrols in two streets in Rome, the rest, they say, are infested by brigands, who attack you at every possible turn. We crossed the St. Angelo bridge, with its great *renaissance* statues by Bernini, black and rugged outlines against the clear, star-lit, bright sky, up to the marvellous piazza before St. Peter's.   The beautiful colonnade which encircles with its arms the immense space of the piazza, the gentle noise made by the falling fountains, a clear sound, only to be heard when everything else is still—seemed so mysterious in the strange starlight !

"When we got out of the carriage, we had to mount the Bernini staircase, with hundreds of steps, flanked by immense pillars.   You cannot imagine what a wonderful, weird-looking place it seemed in that light, with groups of tall men—the Swiss guard—in dresses which rejoiced my heart, invented and designed by Michael Angelo.   At the bottom of the court were the Papal Guards, with flaming cloaks and splendid helmets, also men mounted on very fine horses.

"At the top of the staircase we entered a room with frescos on the walls and ceilings.

"You put aside the huge curtain hung over the entrance door, to get into the Sistine Chapel, which is simple but gorgeous, if you can imagine the combination.

"The wonderful roof, by Michael Angelo, and his fresco of the Last Judgment, which covers the end of the chapel (except where the barbarians cut out a piece for the high altar), half gleams through the blaze of light, not so as to be enjoyed as a picture, but seeming, in a way, to say it was too grand, and well worth being looked at, to be seen through the medium of wax candles.

" The only way to know anything of these frescos is to do as I did the next day. I extended myself at full length on one of the cushioned seats, and, with a powerful opera-glass, enjoyed them at my leisure. I could not leave them for hours, and the consequence is my eyes have ached ever since.

" The screen which divides the chapel is very open, and through it no woman is allowed to pass. Beyond was a perfect blaze of the gold and lace dresses of the different grades of priests, but the chapel has no other ornament than its painted walls and roofs, and massive gold candlesticks.

" I should like to have looked at the whole scene from above, for we must have improved it contrary to the custom of most masses of ladies ; we were all obliged to be dressed in black, with long veils instead of bonnets. It is astonishing how well this mass of black figures (divided from the gentlemen) looked against all the gorgeousness of the chapel and the splendid dresses of the Guards.

" And then the music ! Such curious sounds ; they seemed, somehow, to come straight from the Middle Ages.

" Only vocal music is allowed in the presence of the ' Holy Father,' so you hear nothing but these unusually lovely voices singing difficult and quaint compositions in a marvellous way, as true as if each note were a musical instrument.

"We stayed some time, and then went down the ghostly staircase, with the beautifully dressed men on it, and drove away through the narrow streets to the front of a small café, out of which they brought us cups of chocolate.

"Then we went on to St. Luigi Francese, which much disappointed us—a regular ball-room illumination on the high altar—the most monotonous vespers with organ obligatos, and a tremendous crowd of English sight-seers. It gave me a curious and melancholy feeling of pity for the dull lives of these poor priests, who don't believe half the absurd stories with which they delude the Roman peasantry.

"I must tell you, too, about the wonderful exhibition of the famous Bambino, a little wooden figure, supposed to be blessed with the power of curing any illness—in fact, to be Christ as a baby. This Bambino is a very great personage, and when the Republic was going on they gave it the Pope's grand carriage to go about in and do its miracles with, but when the Pope came back they took away the grand carriage and gave it an ugly old worn-out one instead. We went to see the Bambino at the Ara Cæli. It is put into the middle of a scene like a theatre scene, with the Virgin adoring; a landscape, and in the distance the Magi arriving on horseback, a heavenly host above in the clouds—all lighted up very prettily, and all adoring the Bambino. Opposite this little arrange-ment is a raised platform, where small children stand, and argue points of religion and declaim little set speeches. It was the most absurd *spectacle* I ever saw; they act and they spout the most high-flown spread-eagle sentences, and gesticulate to any extent. This, however, was their kind of argument:

" ' Why was not the Bambino born in the Vatican, as it is such a beautiful place ? '

" ' He might if he liked,' said the other.

" ' Well, why didn't he ? '

" ' Because he was born in a manger to teach us the beautiful virtue of humility.'

"They don't mention the little fact of the Vatican not having been built at that time.

"Some of the figures are made as large as life, and the Christ is said to be cut out of wood from Mount Lebanon. Mr. Howard was in the church when they were arranging the scene, and one man, I suppose a monk, with an eye for arranging tableaux, stood a little way off, saying, ' move that goat '—' put that goat's tail further that way,' etc.

"Our party to see the Vatican by torchlight was a very successful one ; it was a private illumination got up by Mr. Howard and ourselves. We walked about, a ghostly mass, with our torch-bearers in front of us, for two hours among all the wonderful galleries—full of wonders, of which we could only see one or two in each. It was the most beautiful thing I have ever seen in my life.

4*

" The Apollo (except the horrid, modern hands
they have stuck on his beautiful arms) is quite
enough to take your breath away; all the Venuses
in the world sink into insignificance by comparison
with him, and my respect for men has most
strangely risen since I have seen what they might
be, if they were only more like the Apollo.   But
it would take ten letters of ecstatic rapture to give
you an idea of all we saw that night in the Vatican.

" When we came back your little possession
drank four cups of tea, and over-ate herself with
cake and bread and butter.   I should like to return home to you as plump as a little pigeon, and
with life enough in me to scatter into another
world all your horrid *bêtes noires* respecting my
want of strength of mind, or body, for a life with a
limited income.

" Mr. Sedley is in Rome ; do you remember
taking me to his studio in London ?

" I like so to meet people I first saw with you.

" Oh, darling Wil, what a glorious life we shall
have together in the future !   It seems too good
to look forward to, lest it never should be realized.
We are enough and sufficient for ourselves, are we
not, Wil, and not the faintest breath of harm can
touch us from any one but each other.   As for
society and the world—I should like you to see
the inside of my heart for once, and you would see
how callous and indifferent I am, and how I laugh
at the world.

"And now, my own Wil, what wishes can I offer you for the New Year? Only that we may be allowed to end it together in the enjoyment of the peace and great happiness we can make for each other. I hated so to think of you alone on Christmas Day, and I wondered if you were thinking as I was of sweet days to come.

"Ever your loving

"TINY."

CHAPTER XII.

*"Limit your wants: the *Must* is hard, and yet solely by this *Must* can we show how it is with us in our inner man. To live according to caprice requires no peculiar powers."*

GOETHE.

AFTER reading this letter it was natural for Wilfred Lane to believe that Tiny's heart was all his own, and that any sacrifice she would have to make as his wife would be fully recompensed by his devoted affection and their perfect spiritual and intellectual union. Rank and wealth without this would be destitute of all that seemed as necessary to her as the very air she breathed. Such a position would be worse than absolute poverty.

A small house and the difficulty of "keeping down the weekly bills" might, and probably often would, prove distasteful to Tiny; but a marriage which was incomplete and insufficient would be little less than dangerous to a girl of her temperament. Combined with the many good points in Tiny's nature there were evil tendencies of no common strength, and, under such circumstances, these would most assuredly assert themselves.

The thought that, by present rigid economy,

some of Tiny's difficulties in their future home might be diminished, afforded precisely the stimulus Wilfred Lane's own character required.

He was not an idle man, and whilst he keenly appreciated physical ease and all the outward refinements of life, he was very far removed from being a mere pleasure-seeker.

His indifference to money amounted almost to a positive fault, and his carelessness as to his expenditure had on one occasion placed him in a position which he did not scruple to condemn as dishonest as well as dishonorable. It was true that he had not wilfully lived beyond his income like many men, who, for the sake of luxuries they cannot afford, draw bills they know they can never meet, content when the day of reckoning comes to fall back upon "the governor," or to diminish without remorse the slender resources of some indulgent mother, who has to deny herself absolute necessaries in order to pay for extravagance, if not vice.

This Wilfred would have scorned to do.

His humiliation was almost excessive when he found what his easy way of taking things had entailed, and it quite aroused him from indolent but refined enjoyment.

Hitherto his intellectual life had been more dreamy than practical ; now he determined to turn it to better account. It would, however, have taken him some time to extricate himself from a state he regarded with nothing less than abhorrence, but for an unexpected legacy from an old lady to whom his father had rendered an important service. This enabled him to pay off everything without telling his family of his difficulties ; though Lady Harewood often wondered what Wilfred had done with the money, and remarked that he seemed more careful after he had received the thousand pounds than he was before, and never resumed his stall at the Opera, which up to that season he had seldom been without.

All this happened nearly three years before Wilfred fell in love with Tiny ; and though he had somewhat relaxed his literary efforts, he had kept up his reputation as the hardest working man in the War Office.

On his return from Folkestone he had resolved on a winter of real work, during which he would spend as little and earn as much as he possibly could. So he hunted up the editors who had previously employed him ; and being more than usually fortunate, soon found himself in the full swing of work.

He began to feel a very miser ; and when he placed out the money he earned in profitable speculations, he thought of that wonderful story of Silas Marner counting up his heaps of gold ; and felt strangely moved at the remembrance of the old man's despair at losing his money-bags, and his tender, pathetic love for the golden-haired child who strayed into his cottage and reminded him of his lost guineas.

Wilfred said nothing to Tiny about his extra work, and although this incessant occupation certainly helped him to adhere to his plan of writing short letters to Rome, he never put it forward as a reason. He knew very well that he would have written often enough, but for feeling that his restraint better enabled him to keep to the spirit of his sacrifice, and also gave Tiny a fairer opportunity of testing her attachment, than if he fanned the flame already kindled by the constant expressions of his love. Accordingly nearly a fortnight passed before he allowed himself to answer Tiny's last epistle; and the very day on which he meant to write, he received while at breakfast another Roman letter, and during the morning an intimation from Sir Thomas Slade, which would have been a sufficient excuse for writing to Tiny, even if he had posted one the night before.

But we must follow these two events as they happened to Mr. Lane.

CHAPTER XIII.

"Life is good; but not life in itself. So is youth, so is beauty.
 Mere stuff,
"Are all these for Love's usance? To live it is well; but it is
 . not enough.
"Well too, to be fair, to be young; but what good is in beauty
 and youth,
"If the lovely and young are no surer than they that are neither,
 forsooth,
"Young nor lovely, of being beloved? O my love, if thou
 lovest not me,
"Shall I love my own life?"

THE APPLE OF LIFE.

"Thy soul hath snatched up mine, all faint and weak,
 And placed it by thee on a golden throne."

SONNETS FROM THE PORTUGUESE.

"MY OWN WIL,

"I am getting so impatient of this 'eternal city' in spite of all its beauties, that unless you will let me write to you nearly every day, I am sure I shall soon be very ill. I am quite worn out by this continual struggle with the 'interfering atmosphere' we talked about. Not that I am weaker in practice or in feeling; but it is so wearing to force one's self back into one's self, when there are so many influences pulling other ways.

" I daresay you will tell me that it is good for me, and ought to teach me what no one can teach another—how to lead my own life. If I am so weak as to succumb to surrounding influences, there can be no real good in me; and I often think of what you used to say of the amiable weakness which lets people pull you into hourly diversions, and puts an effectual barrier between you and any steady kind of life.

" I feel the want of some hours every day entirely to myself—it seems so necessary and yet so impossible here. It is no joke, this beginning to alter at my time of life; you may laugh, sir, but it is true. All these years in a frivolous worldly atmosphere make a change for the better no quick or easy process.

" Darling Wil, I don't know what benumbing influence has come over me, but I can enjoy nothing, and can hardly take an interest in anything.

" ' An 'orrible tale ' best expresses my condition, ' hypercondriacal, very,'—' the flesh warring against the spirit,' is not a bad quotative description, although not taken from the same original. If I am profane I can't help it. I shall soon be bilious enough to be absolved from all moral responsibility.

" It is not sunrise, but the cocks are crowing so. I love the dicky birds in the garden here, better than anything else in Rome, and the great watchdog that wags its tail at me. But the best wag-

ging comes, however, by the post, though your
letters are so cold that they make me—savagely
longing—especially when I think that we might
have avoided this separation altogether.

" Still, I do think it will be all for the best, if I
only use it rightly. Surely no such pain was ever
sent for nothing ! And it would be utterly unfortunate, if, instead of letting it work its own
good ends, I grew hard and miserable, thinking of
the density and hardness of others. So don't believe that when I *am* good I blame you for sending me to Rome.

"Remember my crack about acquiring experience. I feel such a satisfaction when the pain of
anything turns to an acquired piece of experience
—a greater knowledge of human nature ; it more
than recompenses me for all the suffering. Perhaps I am less sensitive than others, or more
sanguine ; but I have no regrets. If I were a
painter, I would use up my feelings in my pictures
—so much pain to so much canvas !

" It sometimes comes upon me with a rush of
intense feeling, that I have really got you in the
world. The being with you is not all. There is
something in the possession of such a love, and
such a hold in life, however distant ! One is apt
to forget the sweetness of this in the wish for the
entire satisfaction of being with you ; and when
some sign of affection in others, or any little thing
of that sort, recalls that I, too, have a true heart

to depend and lean on—how I wish the feeling
would stop there, but it never does—directly after
comes the yearning and longing, with the dismal
dread lest any misfortunes should prevent these
longings from being eventually fulfilled.

" I think of all kinds of dreadful things, and I
fear them all.

" Yesterday we drove to St. Paolo, about three
miles from here, all through the city, out through
the furthest gate into the country.   Such a strange
drive, through filthy places no one can imagine
who has not been to Rome.   The narrow streets
crowded with peasants, who come in for the *festa*
—very picturesque, but very dirty ; consistent,
very, with the streets, where, at every turn,
through the comical squalid shops and houses,
peep out exquisite pieces of old wall, an old gate-
way, or an old bridge across an alley.

" There is a perfect piece of building left of the
theatre of Marcellus, the arch below being filled
with cheeses, and bunches of carrots hanging
down under the beautiful sculptured stone-work of
the ruin.

" The Church of St. Paolo is the most perfect
thing in or about Rome.   It is hardly yet completed, after about fifty years' hard labor.   All
the Catholic monarchs in Europe have sent
enormous sums and presents for it.   Such pillars I
never saw in my life.   Nothing but one mass of

marble—floor, pillars, and ornaments—very simple, but baffling all description.

" Imagine yourself in the highest building you
ever saw, with vistas of beautiful marble pillars
going off into perspective till they appear quite
tiny, being really so high and massive that human
figures look like insects by them, and all this re-
flected in the beautiful expanse of marble floor.
Such marble, too !   Algerian marble pillars—then
porphyry pillars—malachite in quantities, given by
the Emperor of Russia—and lapis lazuli in such
immense slabs that one can hardly keep up one's
respect for it ; but the balustrades of white Car-
rara marble took my fancy most, with slabs of
beautiful dark-grained porphyry introduced between.

" But all this on paper will not give you the
faintest idea of the simple huge magnificence of the
place, which outside is the most hideous granary-
looking building you can conceive.

" To-day we have been to see an antique statue
in gilded bronze, just discovered under a palace.
The man who found it, and to whom it belonged,
thought he would send it to England and exhibit
it at a guinea a head.   He was dissuaded from
this, and told that English people do not care for
such things, though they make a great fuss about
them when they come out here.   He then offered
it to the Pope, who said he would much like to
have it for the Vatican, but had not a penny he

could call his own to pay for it. So the man magnanimously gave it to the Vatican ; and the Pope made him a marquis, and has given him the monopoly of fish or salt for two years, and taken all the mortgages off his property. Don't they do things absurdly here ?

"And to see the statue ! It is twelve or fourteen feet high, in bronze, covered with gold which is quite bright. It is a Hercules, and very handsome ; but they have not raised him upon his stumps yet (he has not got any feet, at least not on—one is in a corner of the room and the other is in his lion's skin), so he is left lying flat on his back. But the room they have put him in is positively ridiculous. It is all decked out in pink tarlatan, edged with gold tinsel, red cotton velvet —with stars over the walls, and the whole is decorated with the shabbiest of theatre tinsel. I should like you to see the chaste taste of these modern Romans : such an appropriate room for an antique, and all made on purpose !

"THURSDAY.

"We have just had a delicious walk in the Borghese Gardens. This place is a combination of everything that is most delightful in the world. Old statues, lovely fountains, ilex groves, and distant hills. These beautiful things would gladden your eyes and soul ; and I think that of all the delights with which Rome is filled, the Borghese

Gardens have hitherto enchanted me the most.
But in everything one sees there is one great dissatisfaction—such a feeling of what they would all
be, if one could only live in and with them—an
appreciation of what they would be *then*, much
more than the actual pleasure they give one *now*.
Of course this doesn't affect the pictures or
statues so much as the buildings, ruins, and country. I hate all incomplete experience—it leaves
me with such a savage craving !

" I should like to end our days together in
Rome, when you have done grinding at that miserable old War Office ; and, indeed, I often think
you might do many things better for you even
now. My money would go a long way in Rome,
if we lived quietly, and you might be made
Special Correspondent to *The Times*, and all sorts
of things. I am sure this lovely place would fill
you with such fresh and beautiful thoughts that
you would write about them, and gladden the
hearts of those poor souls in dreary, foggy England.

" The very sense of living out here is delicious,
and I am sure you would be a different person if I
could only get you away from the damp climate
and keen winds at home. Yet, to some people,
Rome is very trying ; last week we had a good
deal of rain, with a sirocco wind, and the warm,
dry atmosphere the sirocco brings with it. As a
rule, however, they say the winter here is bright,

clear, and coldish. Certainly, whenever we have
the good fortune to get rid of the sirocco, the
weather is perfect, and the air is so fresh and crisp
that it acts like a tonic.

" And now I must tell you about our presenta-
tion to the Santa Padre, by whom we were
blessed. He is a charming old man, such an in-
ducement to turn Catholic ! We all went dressed
in black, with black lace over our heads. We sat
with some ladies in a long sort of gallery ; then
the Pope came round and spoke to us all, and we
knelt down and kissed his hand. He gave us a
little address, while we continued kneeling ; told
us how much he desired our welfare, and that of
our families and friends, and how earnestly he
hoped we would attend to the affairs of our souls.
Then he blessed us, and a number of rosaries and
other things people had brought, after which he
toddled away. His manner was too sweet !

" The Howards came back with us, and Mr.
Howard told us such a capital story about Captain
———. Queen Victoria honored him with an invitation to Osborne Castle on his return to England after his search for Sir John Franklin in Polar
regions, and he told Lady Franklin afterwards that
he sat by the Princess Royal, and thought her
very odd, for she laughed at nearly every sentence
he uttered. It turned out that Captain —— had
given her good cause to laugh. Not accustomed
to Courts, he had gone to Osborne, oppressed

with the terrible conviction that whenever he
spoke to a royal personage, he must use some formal title ; and, in his absent way, whenever he
spoke to the Princess Royal, he called her ' Your
Holiness.' I think this was enough to upset any
one's gravity. But they say the Queen was very
angry with the Princess for laughing at the poor
man.

" I like Alice Howard extremely ; she is a true-
hearted, nice girl—thoroughly Catholic. I think
all English Catholics have a peculiar manner ;
simple, gentle, and rather up in the clouds, without
being dreamy. There is nothing after all influences people so much as their religion. Don't
you think so ?

" To-morrow we go to the Palazzo Doria.
Sight-seeing is our principal occupation ; and there
is too much variety here in that line, for the others
ever to tire of it, or even to get through it all in
one winter.

" As to society, we know several people now in
Rome, and are constantly seeing them, at our
hotel, or forming parties to visit the churches,
picture-galleries, etc., together in a friendly socia-
ble way ; but I have refused to go to any of the
large receptions. I have too much to do, and feel
too tired to make any efforts to increase my acquaintance ; and the gossiping stories one hears on
all sides, from those who go about a great deal
and make society their principal business, do not

give me a very inviting idea of Roman society, but make me all the more anxious to keep out of the way of it. Madeline and Charlotte are going to two dances in succession early next week ; one at the French Embassy, and the other at the Ashcrofts, who have one of the pleasantest houses here, and receive every Sunday evening.

" Your pretty little friend, Mrs. Willoughby, is here. She has been seriously ill with inflammation of the lungs, but is getting up her strength again now. She is going with us on Saturday for a delightful excursion into the mountains.

" The thing I like best about Rome is getting out of it ; it is cheerful even to play at going away. Oh, Wil, you would not doubt about the future if you could only see into my heart, and find how full it is of you, and know how constantly I long for the presence of the sweet love I want so much. You might well indeed be content. Never have I recognized more than to-day the necessity of your love to make my life complete. I did not know how essential you were to me till I felt what every day increases—the longing for just that one thing which makes life perfect, come what may from the outer world.

"Yes, you dear self-contained old Wil. I don't think you would hesitate to claim your little girl, if you could see for one half minute into her heart of hearts—which is *all* yours.

" Good-by, my own ! Remember a yearning,

5

lonely, wretched, little being, who longs, and longs, and prays, and loves, and does all in fact that such tormented little halved creatures generally do, and all to no purpose.

"Your own, and yours forever,

"TINY.

"P. S.—I send you some little ties which you must wear and fancy yourself at Rome."

CHAPTER XIV.

"Let us be content, in work,
To do the thing we can, and not presume
To fret because it's little."

AURORA LEIGH.

As Wilfred read the last sentence in Tiny's letter he was unpleasantly aroused to a sense of the
flight of time, by the peculiarly loud and unmusi-
cal sound of his landlady's staircase clock; so,
hurriedly thrusting his arms into his coat, he made
his way, regardless of appearances, past Bucking-
ham Palace, through St. James's Square into Pall
Mall.

Wilfred had hardly settled down to his work before he received a summons to his chief's private
room.

When he entered, Sir Thomas Slade was finish-
ing a letter, and looking up hastily, said in a
courteous tone,-"Good morning, Mr. Lane; I
shall be disengaged in a few minutes."

Wilfred sat down by a table on which lay *The
Times;* and, after glancing at the latest telegrams,
he began to speculate in an unusually curious way
upon Sir Thomas Slade's motive for sending for
him.

There was nothing very remarkable in the circumstance after all ; but, somehow or other, Wilfred Lane felt his attendance that morning had not been required in the mere ordinary course of business.   Knowing how little Mr. Chamberlain (Sir Thomas' Private Secretary) had been at the office during the last week, owing to his rapidly failing health, Wilfred began to think Sir Thomas Slade was about to ask him to do some of Chamberlain's work, while the latter took a month's rest at Pau or Mentone—a plan of which he had often talked.

"I sent for you, Mr. Lane," at last began Sir Thomas, laying down his pen, "because I regret to say Mr. Chamberlain is obliged to give up his work altogether.   As the gentleman to whom my secretaryship was promised is unable from private reasons to accept it now, I have much pleasure in offering it to you, having noticed that you are the most careful and accurate man in the office."

"I shall be very glad to accept it, sir," said Wilfred, who was greatly surprised at this stroke of good fortune, "and I feel very grateful for the kind opinion you have expressed, which I hope I may always deserve."

"You must be prepared to enter upon your new duties at once, in fact, this very day ; " and, as he spoke, Sir Thomas pushed a bundle of letters across the table to Wilfred.   "The truth is, poor Chamberlain was not fit for much last week, and these papers have accumulated in consequence. You will find my notes on the back of each; be good enough to carry out my instructions, and, when you observe a cross at the end of my memoranda, you may know I wish to sign the letter myself, it must therefore be written accordingly. I daresay for the next day or two you will meet with several signs which will puzzle you; get through the work which is plain, and then come to me with any requiring explanation. . I shall expect a little extra interruption at first."

After a few more directions, Sir Thomas desired Mr. Lane to take possession of Mr. Chamberlain's room, and informed him that his additional salary would commence from that day.

When Wilfred found himself fairly installed in Mr. Chamberlain's place, it was contrary to human nature to expect he should think of another man's misfortunes, rather than of the good which they had been the means of bringing him.

Here, indeed, was a sudden rise, and an utterly unexpected one.

His work would of course be considerably heavier, and far more onerous; but an extra salary of £250 a year made the former sink into insignificance, and the latter he contemplated with unmitigated satisfaction. Now, he thought, he should have an opportunity of proving his real value, and this secretaryship might, perhaps, lead to some ultimate advancement.

Wilfred Lane knew his own powers, and felt

they could be much better employed in the public
service, in positions of greater trust than the one
he had previously occupied.   Possessing an evenly
balanced mind, without any tendency to conceit
or self-assertion, he was able to estimate his own
capabilities, without over-rating or unduly depre-
ciating them.

It is quite as impossible for a man of real power
to be unconscious of it, as it is for a woman to be
ignorant of her beauty and personal attractions.

A thoroughly educated man, in the fullest sense
of the word, Wilfred knew what faculties he possessed, and the uses to which he could best apply
them—the first step to enable an individual to act
wisely in any station of life.   But he had also realized one of the last—the significance of almost
every act of a man's daily life, in its ultimate oper-
ation on himself and others ; and, having naturally
a very strongly marked character, his gentleness
and modesty shone out with an unusual grace, for
these qualities were in keeping, as they always
must be, with the largeness of his apprehension
and his perception of the infiniteness of the things
he could never know.

The first day's work in his new position did not
prove a light one.   It was, indeed, true that,
owing to Mr. Chamberlain's illness and irregular
attendance, all the less pressing letters had been
laid aside until they had accumulated into a very
formidable heap.   Wilfred was busy over them,

when he was surprised by a kind letter from Mr. Chamberlain, saying how glad he was to hear that Lane was his successor. Had he been able to leave home he should have looked in, to explain the way in which he left Sir Thomas Slade's papers. Should Lane, however, require any information, and think it worth his while to call, he knew where to find him.

Wilfred was pleased with Mr. Chamberlain's letter, which gave him the opportunity of calling as soon as he left the War Office. But he could not wait till then, and lose a day's post, before he despatched a note to Rome to tell Tiny of his appointment. If he had hitherto restrained his feelings when he wrote, in accordance with his resolution, there was no reason to deprive her of the pleasure of hearing, as soon as possible, of a promotion which would, at any rate, make their marriage a degree less difficult than it seemed after that fearful talk with Lady Harewood, when his "miserable prospects" and "uncertain health" were so vividly brought before him.

As Wilfred recalled that afternoon he could not help feeling heartily glad that he owed his present appointment, not to private interest, but to the reasons assigned by Sir Thomas Slade. Above all, he congratulated himself that he was by no means indebted to his aunt for it. Lady Harewood had made him sensible of former obligations in a manner which did a great deal towards lessening the gratitude he would otherwise have felt, and raising in its place a devout hope that she would in future refrain from bestowing any favor upon him.

So a few lines were scribbled off to Tiny, to convey the good news, and assure her that her descriptions of Rome were glorious, and the sight of her yellow envelopes the only things which gave him any real pleasure. He hoped soon to see another; and promised to answer one and all in a way which would thoroughly satisfy her when she returned home; but at present she must take for granted all her own heart disposed her to wish for. She could not take more than he was ready to give. During the next few days Wilfred had enough to do. He was anxious not to get in arrears with his literary work. He knew, when once he had mastered the accumulated papers, his official employment would not interfere with the engagements he had made in other directions; and he was bent on leaving no stone unturned, both to make and save money enough to furnish a comfortable little home for Tiny, so that, when Lady Harewood gave her consent, they would be in a position to make a clear start upon their mutual income.

With the money inherited from his mother, his increased salary at the War Office, and the proceeds of his writings, Wilfred Lane already possessed an income of eight hundred pounds a year.

It was true that his secretaryship was not a permanent one, and there were chances which might curtail the income derived from other sources, but he was in a very hopeful mood, and, in the face of his present good fortune, not disposed to take a melancholy view of affairs in general, or his pecuniary concerns in particular.

Tiny was ill in bed when the letter containing the news of Wilfred's appointment reached her. The coming illness upon which she had fathered her melancholy tendency to " profanity " had already arrived, not however as a bilious attack, but in the shape of a severe cold. Indeed, poor Tiny had not left her room since the day on which she posted her last letter.

Her delight at hearing of the secretaryship was as great as if Wilfred had been made Governor-General of India. She knew the addition to his salary would be nothing in Lady Harewood's eyes ; and that it would take a very different kind of appointment to reconcile her to the proposed marriage ; but she resolved to act as if she thought her mother would offer no opposition, if Wilfred possessed anything like a respectable income. Although Tiny was unable to include the result of Wilfred's literary work (for the simple reason that she knew nothing about it), she considered his present salary, joined to her income, sufficient to begin with, and to provide a modest establishment with the " bare necessaries of life."

5*

Not that Tiny Harewood's ideas upon the subject of money had any sound basis. She knew, indeed, that she could not keep her own expenses within bounds, but often borrowed from her sisters, to help her on to the next quarter; even at the present moment she had two advances to repay, as well as several outstanding bills. This, however, only presented to Tiny's mind a temporary difficulty, which would never occur in the future. She was even now " economizing " (according to *her* sense of the word) to pay off these sums; and, as they had been spent in luxuries she ceased to value with their possession, she felt it would be easy to avoid ever again placing herself in a similar position.

But Tiny's views upon expenditure were so exceedingly vague, that as far as any executive faculty was concerned, she was (with the best intentions) utterly unfit to be a poor man's wife. Large sums of money would disappear before she was conscious of it; for acute, clever, and observant as Tiny was in most things, pounds, shillings, and pence had no power to make a mental impression upon her. Certainly, she had never yet tried to cultivate a better understanding between her purse and her expenditure, but habitually fell back upon her sisters' good-natured practice of keeping not only her accounts, but her quarterly money; the latter was never confided to Tiny until a good number of bills from the various dressmakers, jewellers, and dry-goods stores patronized by the little spendthrift were systematically collected and paid by Madeline for the credit of the family.

Even then this wilful little individual refused to inspect the several items; and, while she laughingly complained of any reduction in the money she expected to receive, she resolutely declined to believe in the sum total of the paid-up accounts.

All this, however, and a great deal more, Tiny intended to alter when she married. As Mrs. Wilfred Lane she had unbounded faith in her power of looking through the unpleasant red and blue books containing butchers', bakers', and grocers' weekly accounts; and she determined to commence her duties by purchasing a complete set of housekeeping books, which she had seen in a shop in Bond Street, handsomely bound in green morocco with gold clasps, and standing in an appropriately expensive case.

CHAPTER XV.

"Life treads on life, and heart on heart,
We press too close in church and mart
To keep a dream or grave apart."

A VISION OF POETS.

THE first person to whom Tiny communicated the news of Wilfred's appointment, was Madeline; she was always sure of a certain amount of sympathy from her sister Madeline; whose sweetness of disposition and natural goodness of heart made it easy for her to enter into the feelings of others, and rendered it quite impossible for her to banish all interest in her cousin, because she objected to his marriage with Tiny, though of course she wished Wilfred had not fallen in love with her sister, and would have esteemed him more highly had he yielded at once to family opposition.

Besides a strong personal liking for Wilfred, which had grown up during childhood (much of which had been spent together), and, in addition to many points of sympathy, Madeline had another link with her cousin. Wilfred had often been accompanied by his friend, Captain Grahame, in his visits to the Harewoods; and, though no definite words of love had ever passed his lips, a secret understanding existed between Arthur Grahame and Madeline; she knew that she was loved, and gave him her heart in return.

When Arthur Grahame's regiment was ordered to the Crimea, Madeline was with some friends in the North of Ireland; but a message, sent in the farewell letter he wrote to Lane from Portsmouth, fortunately betrayed his secret to Wilfred; and it was due to her cousin's thoughtful tenderness, that the sad news that Arthur Grahame had been one of the first to fall at the storming of the Redan, was broken to her at a time when her sorrow could find free vent. Although Madeline had never openly acknowledged to Wilfred how much she loved his friend, his exquisite tact and delicacy enabled her to talk freely of Arthur; and she received from him a silent sympathy, which, perhaps, possessed greater healing power than any spoken words.

Time had done its work in restoring Madeline to serenity and cheerfulness; but sometimes her sorrow still asserted itself; and then the remembrance of what Wilfred Lane had been to her in the hour of need came back with such force that she felt herself a traitor in opposing his marriage, and sometimes almost determined to desert her mother and Charlotte, and to go over openly to the enemy.

But, if she wavered in giving Wilfred and Tiny

a steady outward adherence, she certainly could not refrain from rejoicing in her heart at any good fortune which tended to promote the fulfilment of their wishes; and accordingly she was as much pleased as even the exacting Tiny could desire, at hearing of her cousin's appointment.

While they were talking over the matter, Lady Harewood's near approach was announced by the peculiar rustling of her stiff silk dress ; and, as the door slowly opened, the very air itself seemed to lose its light and pleasant qualities and to become charged with explosive elements.

Lady Harewood's entrance always acted as a spell upon her daughters ; the tone of their voices was not only lowered, as she touched the outer handle of the door, but the conversation entirely ceased, and was seldom resumed until after her exit, and then generally in a different spirit, and in another key.

Yet it was scarcely poor Lady Harewood's fault. She was not exactly unkind to her children. She was naturally a fretful woman, with irritable nerves; and her daughters' earnestness and animation probably grated as much upon her sensibilities as her own die-away lachrymose manners annoyed and *crispèd* them. But, whatever may have been the cause, the fact remained the same ; and a want of sympathy existed between them, which doubtless produced bad effects upon them all, and deprived the domestic circle of that cordiality and freedom which alone entitles a household to the sacred name of *home*.

The polite inquiries which Lady Harewood made respecting Tiny's health were chilling in themselves, from a mother's lips.

After they were satisfactorily answered, Tiny (who was generally in the extreme of either leaving her mother altogether in the dark about her concerns, or else doing battle over them in a somewhat too vigorous style) commenced the remark she intended to make at the first opportunity :

" I have just had a letter from Wilfred. Sir Thomas Slade has made him his secretary, which gives him another £250 a year, so now we have plenty to marry upon."

Lady Harewood expressed herself duly interested in hearing the news, and showed by sundry signs and innuendoes that she was even prepared to read her nephew's letter ; but, gathering from Tiny's manner that this unwonted exertion would be denied her, she refrained from directly asking for the epistle.

"It cannot be a permanent appointment," was her freezing remark; "and as the Ministry is nearly sure to go out early in the spring, you had better advise Wilfred to make hay while the sun shines, for it will not last very long."

" I don't see that at all," rejoined Tiny ; "and anyhow it will probably lead to something better.

People like Sir Thomas Slade are fortunately able
to appreciate something out of the common way
when they have the good luck to meet with it."

" I dare say your cousin is a very clever young
man," rejoined her mother, " but he is exceedingly opinionated ; and I cannot say I think as highly
of him as I did."

" Then I am sorry for you, mamma," said Tiny,
raising herself up in her bed, her face flushing
with excitement. " It is a pity that Wilfred ever
made such a noble sacrifice of his own wishes, if
you are incapable of appreciating it. I always
told him it would do no good."

" I don't understand what you mean about 'sacrifice : ' if I chose to come to Rome with your sisters, it was neither possible for you to remain
behind, nor for Wilfred to accompany us. It was
a great mistake ever to allow that young man to
make himself so completely at home in my
house."

" Why, mamma," exclaimed Tiny, " it was
Wilfred himself who proposed your bringing me
to Rome ; and as for his coming to our house, he
is the best man who ever entered it since poor
papa died."

Lady Harewood was exceedingly glad that the
latter part of Tiny's speech gave her an opportunity of evading any further discussion upon
Wilfred's share in the visit to Rome. She
therefore contented herself with rebuking Tiny for

comparing any one to her revered father; and condemned the allusion to Sir Henry as undutiful, disrespectful, and wanting in all proper feeling towards herself. Seeing that Tiny was fast losing all self-control, and anticipating an angry scene, Lady Harewood veered towards the door; and had almost left the room before she concluded her sentence. She saw by the kindling fire in Tiny's eye, and the nervous movement of her hands, that she stood small chance of the last word, unless content to drop her assumed manners—exert her voice to an unwonted pitch—and to exchange her usually languid tone for something more natural though less polite.

Relieved of her mother's presence, Tiny began to cry. She felt ill, wretched, and hated these contests. She had no intention of saying anything disrespectful to anybody when she began talking; and she was sure that she had said nothing wrong about her father, for whose memory her reverence was extreme.

But her conscience did not feel so clear about her mother; and the sense of the indignation with which she regarded her at that moment, grated against the finer chords of Tiny's character, until the whole seemed to strike a discord.

These were some of the moments when Tiny longed most for Wilfred. She would tell him all the little perplexities and fights which went on in her own mind; and while he never scrupled to

blame her for want of self-control, he always
soothed and entered into the intense provocation
produced on a girl of Tiny's temperament by contact with a nature like her mother's—a provocation
which Tiny would have felt had Lady Harewood
only been a person in whose society she was
thrown ; but which was roused to an unendurable
pitch by the very fact of their close relationship.

After these scenes Tiny was occasionally like a
little mad creature ; her nerves seemed all un-
strung, her physical condition thoroughly dis-
ordered, and she appeared unable to subdue any
sentiment which came first to the surface.

On the present occasion the discussion was
fortunately cut so short that a few moments
sufficed to restore her to calmness; and she determined to soothe her ruffled plumes by inditing
a letter of congratulation to Wilfred.

CHAPTER XVI.

"In the ardor of passion they deceive themselves; how then can we help being deceived by them?"

GOETHE.

"MY DEAREST WILFRED,

"Your letter has just arrived, and it is the nicest I have ever received from you, although it only contains fifty-one words, for I have counted them twice over!

"I am so delighted with dear old Sir Thomas Slade; I could hug him, and I would, too, if he would only give you an order to write a long letter to me at least once a week, as the first and most important duty of your new appointment. I am sure he would be horrified if he knew how badly you treat me. I don't believe you care a straw for me now, or you could not help saying something loving and kind in your letters. I daresay you pretend that your feelings are too tender for paper. Remember '*les extrêmes se touchent.*' I shall be thinking the unfeeling 'extreme' is the cause of your silence, if something pretty does not come soon. I want a great deal, and much which I cannot have till I get home.

When I think of getting back to you my heart and head get dizzy with delight, for I am so lonely.

" I have just had a scene with mamma, which makes me long more and more to be with you, in the little home we pictured together, that happy afternoon in the Square gardens. I feel so drearily weary of this solitude ; and the contrast of the quietness, without the solitude, strikes one vividly. Such a home would fill life with sweet hours—hours which would give me strength for any amount of work and goodness.

.   .   .   .

" Miss Barclay has just been here. She came up and stayed an hour with me. First, she talked about Mrs. Browning, whom she knew intimately ; and ranks next to Shakespeare, and above Tennyson—far. She told me she considered it something in her life to have known such a person ; that while you were with her, it was impossible to have a low or worldly thought ; she lived in a higher, purer atmosphere than most people ; and was, altogether, even out of her poetry, the most wonderful creature Miss Barclay ever knew. After saying much more than I can write, she read from Mrs. Browning's last volume ' Bianca and the Nightingales ; ' and then took up our favorite Sonnets from the Portuguese, and read them through from beginning to end. To say she reads perfectly is poor praise compared to what she deserves.

"When she came to ours—do you remember it? (if not, look at your book and the mark I have added to your old date)—it seemed so wrong for any lips but yours to read to me—' *How do I love thee, let me count the ways!* '·

"Yes, darling Wil, I can't stand this much longer. I shall become really sick if I stay out here. I feel utterly miserable now. The air is so sweet that it is desperately melancholy work to feel ill and weary in such a place. To complete my unhappy state, there is a harmony flute playing melancholy Verdi through the soft sunny spring air. You strong-nerved old Wil, do you think that nonsense?

. . . .

" I have been to sleep, and I think I feel better! My little bow-wow Tip is on his arm-chair close beside me ; he tells me to say that he would like to bite you for not writing longer letters to me, and is much surprised that you have never inquired after him.

. . . .

" Here goes over all the ink! That's a judgment on me, either for repeating Tip's impertinence, or for quarrelling with mamma. Wil, in spite of the ink, I really think things look a little brighter for my sleep. Madeline says mamma will be sure to leave Rome after the 'Carnival ; and if she does not go to Naples (which is every day getting more and more likely), we shall come straight home.

" I think I must belong in some measure to the Salamandrine type, or I should not have had such a cruel trial as this sent me ; but, having you for a support, I should be wicked if I let it harden me.

" No, we are given the materials for making our own moral sunshine, and make it we will ! This must be the end of our troubles. No more suffering, save what we bring on ourselves, or what comes direct from the hand of God.

" How delicious to think of your new appointment. With this extra two hundred and fifty pounds we shall have plenty of money.

" Madeline tells me to finish this directly, or I shall lose the post. I wish I had gone on writing to you, instead of going to sleep, spilling the ink, and listening to Miss Barclay's reading.

" Good-by, my own Wil, I shall make haste and learn how to become a good little wifie.

> " ' I will not be proud of my youth or my beauty,
> Since both of them wither and fade,
> But gain a good name by well doing my duty :
> This will scent like a rose when I'm dead.'

" A little effusion from Dr. Watts, the effect of trying to strengthen my memory !

" Your loving

" Tiny."

Inside the envelope was a little note, which Madeline had slipped in unknown to her sister,

not only to congratulate Wilfred upon his good
fortune, but to ask him to do his best to cheer up
Tiny. "She wants moral tone," wrote Madeline,
"and ought to be made to feel that another
month's separation is not a lifetime. I know
enough of low spirits, myself, to feel very much
for the dear child, and to wish her to be gently
dealt with ; but don't let her spoil her visit to
Rome with pining, and making herself ill, if you
can help it."

Wilfred felt very anxious when he read this
note. He feared Tiny must indeed be depressed,
before Madeline would so far acknowledge his
position, as to apply for his influence.

Under these circumstances he thought himself
entitled to write a loving letter. He could not
bear the idea that he was withholding what Tiny
so sorely needed. It was bad enough to have
sent her away at all ; and he felt strongly tempted
to break through his resolutions, to write fully and
freely from the depth of his heart, and to pour
forth all the love he had been storing up during
these dreary weeks.

So he wrote, and urged Tiny to keep well and
strong for his sake ; to remember her promise of
coming back as "plump as a pigeon ; " and threatened to break down in his new work, unless speedily assured of her convalescence. He spoke of
having got through the worst part of the time, and
said he hoped she would scarcely be able to write

another letter without telling him something definite about her return home ; and then he could not refrain from adding : " Would to God I could tell you in words one half I feel for you. You little know how I long for the time when my darling will be indeed, and in very truth, my own. Your little moans for my love are painfully precious to me. God hasten the day, sweet one, after which you shall never look in vain for it. Your weary lonely feeling will be, I trust, forever satisfied when I have my own ' little sunshine ' in arms which long to enclose her. The future holds but one thing in it to

" Yours ever,

" WILFRED LANE."

CHAPTER XVII.

" Better trust all, and be deceived,
And weep that trust, and that deceiving;
Than doubt one heart, that, if believed,
Had blessed one's life with true believing.
" Oh, in this mocking world, too fast
The doubting fiend o'ertakes our youth !
Better be cheated to the last,
Than lose the blessed hope of truth."

FRANCES A. KEMBLE.

WHEN Tiny received this letter she jumped about for very joy.

Knowing Wilfred's determination of character, and his resolution to say nothing in his letters but what a cousin might write, she felt his love for her must indeed be deep and strong, for this expression of it to have escaped him. Of course she did not know that Madeline had written; for Wilfred gathered from his cousin's way of wording her note, that he was not to mention finding it in Tiny's envelope.

She sent this answer by the same day's post.

6

"OH! YOU DEAREST OLD BOY,

"I am so glad I have hunted you down from your pedestal, and made you say one lover-like thing at the last gasp!

"The others have all gone to the Vatican; and I was staying at home by myself, when your dear letter was brought in. When I read it, I was so glad I was alone.

"I wish you would always write to me what passes in that great heart of yours; for I cannot help thinking our future happiness depends on our being one, as much as possible, during this horrible separation. My letters would be altogether filled with what concerns you and me, only you told me to tell you of all I do and see. But, though life is so full, and there is so much going on around me, when the day is over, with its astonishingly beautiful sights, I feel the awful want of my own true love to soothe me, and to gloss over everything in life with his tenderness. Your absence is more a want at the root of life than an absolute active pain.

"I went to a French service yesterday in a Lutheran chapel, and liked the sermon very much, because it reminded me of what you had been to me. The text was from that chapter where Elijah goes into the desert in a state of despondency, and says, 'It is enough, O Lord; now take away my life, for I am no better than my fathers.'

"The sermon was on the moments of despond-

ency which come to every one, almost—either
from great moral pain, or from emptiness in life,
and the feeling of self-detestation, or from the
higher impulses never being satisfied—being con-
tradicted, in fact, by our habits. And how all
this dissatisfaction encrusts life with a melancholy
in the soul, which brings at last all who live in
and for the world to the state when death seems
the only outlet for their misery. He described
most wonderfully the feeling which the suppression
of all high motives to action produces. I could
not help thinking of last year, when I was so miserable, and prayed for an influence strong enough
to take me out of the melancholy of an excited,
vapid life; and how you, my own strong Wil, effected what no saint, angel, or anything else good
and human, could have done.

"I wonder whether I shall ever be able to tell
you all that passes in my little person? If you
were Father Confessor to me, as well as the many
other things you are, it might be well! I cannot
help thinking it would be good to recognize in
words, and to another—such another as you are to
me—all the shortcomings of one's thoughts.

"Oh, Wil, the world is a funny place—and it is
made so strange by these queer hearts of ours.

"There are certain faults which are scarcely
recognizable, and yet they eat into the very character; and, more or less, this makes the world at
core a very lying, deceptive one. There are few

if any saints in it after all! There are many pas-
sionless, feelingless, otherwise good people who
pass for such; but who knows what calm lives
have been allotted them? I don't know why I am
writing this homily to you. But I feel very
stupid. What does it matter? my old Wil must
have me—stupid or otherwise—just as he finds
me. He has promised to take me, for better for
worse, and he can't alter, however idiotic I become!

" Your loving

" TINY."

There was something in the tone of this letter
which Wilfred could not understand, and which he
did not altogether like. Was it possible that
Tiny, who appeared so frank and open, and who
seemed as if she could not keep the smallest secret
to herself—was it possible that she would hide
thoughts and feelings which she knew would cause
him pain, and perhaps displeasure? Wilfred dismissed this idea as ridiculous. Did he not know
Tiny from beginning to end—had she not often
told him that no one in the world understood her
but himself?

What *could* Tiny have to hide from him?
Nothing surely but feelings which, as a wife, she
would gladly confide to him; but which, divided
as they were, it was only natural she should retain
in her own bosom. He ought to be satisfied, and

he was satisfied with the frank and free expression she now gave to her affection for him. The rest would all come in the happy future, which Wilfred so often pictured, as he walked back from his office ; and he sighed for the time when, instead of going to his chambers, he should hasten towards a real home, and be greeted by a fair young wife who promised to bring him such peace and happiness in the future.

Had Wilfred been less occupied, he might have dwelt upon Tiny's expressions more than he did : but life was very full to him, and, though his whole heart was centred in her, other interests claimed so much of his time that he was prevented from following out the train of thought which this letter at first suggested.

CHAPTER XVIII.

" Till I press thee against my heart—my wife—
(Come thou wilt, tho' I know not when)
While I bide my time, thus I'll live my life,
Aye, my love I will keep till then."

Semper Fidelis.

LADY HAREWOOD *was* at last fairly tired of
Rome ; and, having spent a great deal more money
than she intended, did not care to go to Naples.

After all, she had been away from England
for four months. It was not to be supposed she
should inconvenience herself for the sake of keeping Wilfred and Tiny apart for the exact time suggested. Besides which, an earlier return would
enable her to take up a position for which her
nephew would be unprepared, and of which she
determined to say nothing till she reached Grosvenor Crescent.

When Tiny heard that they were going direct
to London, her delight knew no bounds. She regarded the visit to Rome as the term of her separation from Wilfred : and, being innocent of
Lady Harewood's further plot against their happiness, she believed the barrier to their union would
now be removed. So, a few days after Wilfred

had received the letter, which caused him the
speculations already recorded, the long-expected
tidings of Tiny's speedy return gladdened his
eyes.

"ROME.

"Oh, Wilfred, I could sing with joy! What a
blessing it is that everybody isn't like you. Had
you come to Rome instead of remaining in London, I suppose nothing on earth would have induced such a precise old monster to leave it a
moment before the cruel six months had expired;
you obstinate, hard-hearted man!

"At last I have something 'definite' to tell you
of our return. Mamma has determined on going
straight to London; and has ordered us to get our
heavy luggage ready for forwarding, as soon as
ever we can. So now I will go on to tell you of
the proceedings of a no longer dreary little person; but of one who is filled with delight at the
thought of being able soon to extort all you have
promised to give in answer to letters, which have
been received with a coolness and want of thankfulness for which you shall most certainly be
called to account.

"Well, our expedition to Frascati was delightful. It was a great success, and we did it in all
completeness. The views were quite beyond description beautiful, in their own line. We drove
all day in two vehicles, one a large open omnibus,
and the other an ordinary carriage.

"We lunched all together on a green, sunny corner of a vineyard, and came home from Albano by train, reaching this at half-past eight o'clock.

"The sunset over the Campagna was something too exquisite. My own Wil; we *must* come and wander among these mountains together; they are so beautiful.

"But I can't write. I can only think of seeing dear old London again, with its ugly houses and dull streets and squares.

"I have been trying to read Ruskin, but even that I could not do—for a dear face and its wicked brown eyes would come between me and the pages. I did enjoy though, immensely, a little bit of his about the pines. Do you remember it? And then about the flowers; how and why the greatest masters didn't paint much for the sake of flowers, explaining what I have often felt about them—the limited definite feeling they leave. They want the closest attention; but when you have given that you know all—there is no further mystery.

"Flowers, he says, seem intended for the solace of ordinary humanity. Children love them; quiet, tender, contented, ordinary people love them as they grow; luxurious people rejoice in them gathered. Passionate or religious minds contemplate them with fond, feverish intensity; the affection is seen severely calm in the works of many old religious painters. To the child and the

girl, the peasant and the manufacturing operative,
to the grisette and the nun, the lover and the
monk, they are always precious. But to the men
of supreme power and thoughtfulness, precious
only at times ; symbolically and pathetically often
to the poets, but rarely for their own sake. They
fall forgotten from the great workmen's and soldiers' hands. Such men will take in thankfulness
crowns of leaves or crowns of thorns—not crowns
of flowers. And then he tells a lovely story of
his friend who went with him into the Tyrol one
early spring and saw a strange mountain in the
distance, belted, he thought, about its breast with a
zone of blue, which turned out to be a belt of gen-
tians, which, as they approached, expanded into
a richer breadth and heavenlier blue.

" It is such a strange effect reading Ruskin with
the window open—a lovely, balmy, spring feeling in
the air—and the sounds of all this idiotic Carnival
going on in the distance—guns firing for the races,
and the noise of a crowd all over the place. We
had a number of friends in our balcony this morning, throwing sugar-plums at the people in the
street below ; I think the Carnival stupid beyond
description ; and how men can make such fools of
themselves, for ten of God's whole days, baffles
my comprehension.

" Now that this separation is nearly over, I
almost feel able to say that I am glad I came.
What you are to me I should never have known

6*

without it ; and this shows me how utterly I belong to your life—*our* life—our sweet life, out of
the world, all to ourselves. It is a future to live
for ! But I shan't feel safe till I am really with
you. The slightest thing amiss, and I directly
think of the dear, strong arm which makes everything so easy to bear. I broke a looking-glass
the other day, and that is so dreadfully unlucky !
I hope nothing will happen ; and assuredly it well
might, for the delight of leaving here so soon is
too much for me.

"It is so delicious to think I may begin to say,
with some idea of its being true, ' to-day is the last
Monday in Rome.'

"At the Vespers, yesterday, I pitied all the
poor old priests and monks, who will go on sitting
in their places for ever so long, without any Wil
(or its equivalent) to go to. But I am getting
maudlin !

"I have splendid plans for the future, and intend to lead such a regular life. It shall be a
religion to get up early ; my physical strength
will be devoted to those things you have taught
me to love ; and my moral strength to make you
happy. So you see Rome is very little to me
now, one way or another. I am only thinking of
this day fortnight. Good-by, my own Wil ; prepare yourself for no end of torment from yours,
now and forever,

"TINY."

After this Wilfred heard no more until he received a little hurried scrap, dated *Hotel Westminster, Paris*, which told him that the Harewoods expected to arrive at the Charing Cross station on the following Thursday night, at twenty-five minutes to eleven o'clock, if trains and steamers did their duty, and brought them as quickly as Tiny wished to come.

CHAPTER XIX.

"Expecting joy is a happy pain."

ADELAIDE A. PROCTER.

THE clock was striking half-past ten as Wilfred
Lane walked into the Charing Cross station.
Making his way at once to the platform, he awaited
the arrival of the tidal train from Folkestone.

Of course, it was late that night; and as Wilfred
impatiently paced up and down, the idea of seeing
Tiny again began to feel like a dream. It almost
seemed a trick of his imagination; and he half
expected, when the train disgorged its occupants,
that no Tiny Harewood would be found among
the travellers. As he took her note out of his
pocket to reassure himself, Lady Harewood's carriage drove into the station, in evident anticipation
of what was to come.

In a few minutes the railway officials began to
collect, and the approach of the train was so
clearly indicated that Wilfred thought by the time
he had taken one walk down the length of the
platform, his waiting would be over.

He had nearly reached the furthest end, when

he heard a quick step behind him, and the familiar voice of Lady Harewood's footman accosted him with the pleasant sound—

" The train is just coming in, sir."

As the man spoke, it slowly steamed into the station, with a puff, puff, puff, which sounded very differently in Wilfred's ears to that horrible grating sound the steamer had made at the Folkestone pier four months ago.

Tiny Harewood was eagerly looking out of the window, and caught sight of Wilfred long before the train stopped. The carriage which contained this precious treasure passed him, though he had rapidly walked to the other end of the platform ; but it was scarcely this which made his heart beat loud and fast.

By the time he reached Tiny's carriage a porter had already opened the door, and before Wilfred knew what was going to happen, regardless of the crowd around her, or the presence of her mother and sisters, Tiny sprang into his arms, and gave him an embrace, which not only took him completely by surprise, but knocked his hat off, much to the annoyance of an irascible old gentleman who immediately put his foot through it, and considered himself the aggrieved party.

As Wilfred Lane handed Lady Harewood into what her daughters always called the " family hearse," he felt somewhat discomposed, for he was averse to public exhibitions of affection. The meeting had been so sudden, and the unfortunate hat had taken such a prominent part in it, that he found it impossible to exchange a word with Tiny. Now he must say " Good-night," for John and the maid had discovered the luggage, and there was nothing more to detain his aunt.

" I am very glad to see you back again," said Wilfred, speaking to Lady Harewood, but holding Tiny's hand firmly in his; " I hope you will let me look in to-morrow at five o'clock, aunt.

" Certainly," she replied, in a formal tone, which augured ill for the future happiness of the young lovers; "what I have to say to you, Wilfred, might just as well be said at once."

" Good-night, Wil," said Tiny; "I am so happy. To-morrow at five o'clock!   Don't be late," she added; and the carriage drove off before Wilfred had time to reply save by an extra pressure of the little hand he had held captive during this conversation.

John disappeared with his mistress, and Mr. Lane found the maid still struggling with the luggage, which had yet to be put on her cab. She was very grateful for his assistance, and the porters seemed much more willing and brisk now they had a gentleman to look after them and the hope of a " tip " at the end of their labors.

Mrs. Smith was not only fatigued with the journey, and incensed with John, who ought, in her opinion, to have kept Lady Harewood waiting till he saw the luggage on the cab, but she was smarting under the sense of a deeper wrong.

It was, in her opinion, a great deal too bad of Lady Harewood to have parted with her courier in Paris. She felt personally aggrieved by being obliged to travel " such a distance alone, with so many changes, and some, too, amongst foreign tongues ; " it was a position which she considered unbecoming to her ladyship and most derogatory to herself. Being left by John before the cab was ready to start was the " last drop in her cup," and she determined to speak very frankly on the subject to Mr. Watson, as soon as ever she found her self in the housekeeper's room in Grosvenor Crescent.

" If gentlefolks wished to keep up to their station," she intended to remark, " they should behave different before a whole train load of people, not to reckon the steamer, who might any day turn out to be the nobility of their own circle."

" Law, Mr. Lane, excuse me, sir," said Mrs. Smith, when she found herself comfortably settled in the cab, with the luggage piled up over her head, and the seats crammed with the small bags and wraps which had all been left by the offending John ; " but what has happened to your hat ? You can never walk through the streets with it, sir."

" Well, I don't think many people will notice it at this time of night," said Mr. Lane, laughing, as

he told the cabman where to drive, and, with a
friendly good-night to Smith, whom he envied from
the bottom of his heart when he thought how soon
she would see Tiny, while he had to wait till five
o'clock to-morrow afternoon, he watched the cab
rattle out of the station, and walked thoughtfully
back to his own chambers.

There was something unpleasant in the ring of
Lady Harewood's voice, he thought, and the manner in which she answered his request for leave to
call on the following day. Was it possible that
she meant to oppose him still? Had Tiny been
right in her conjecture that her mother avoided a
distinct promise with a view to this?

If so, what could he do—what ought he to do?
He could no longer doubt Tiny's love. She had
stood the test of a long separation, and the greet-
ing she had given him at the station was assurance
enough that he had her whole heart, and that she
did not mind who knew it. Wilfred Lane had
been quite unprepared for such a demonstration,
and would certainly have preferred a less public
embrace. Still, as a proof of Tiny's thorough devotion to him, the remembrance of it was very
precious.

But when he reached his lodgings he was obliged
to dismiss anxious as well as sweet thoughts, for
he had some work which he knew must be done
that night. Exchanging his coat for a loose dress-
ing-gown, he banked up his fire, lighted his pipe,

and spreading out his papers on the table before him, worked away for some hours.

Although not a strong man, Wilfred Lane had a wonderful capacity for being able to do with very little sleep. After a night's work (and sometimes a night's illness) which would have sent many a stronger man to his office with a headache and pale face, he would look as bright as usual after his morning bath and breakfast. This constant want of sufficient rest was beginning to make him seem older than he really was, and perhaps added to the already deeply-marked lines on his brow, but otherwise it did not appear to tell upon him. His general health had certainly rather improved of late, and his heart attacks had been far less frequent and severe.

Over and above the delight of knowing that every hour's labor would contribute to Tiny Harewood's future ease and comfort, Wilfred Lane loved his work for its own sake. He was passionately devoted to subjects of thought out of the beaten line of the day ; and he had naturally an ardent impulse for seeking the genuine truth on all matters, and the gift of finding and recognizing it when found. The impulse for seeking truth is perhaps more common than we think—the gift of finding it much rarer.

But his line of activity was in " the war for the liberation of humanity," as Goethe calls it. To help forward by unceasing efforts all schemes connected with education, all things likely to promote a wider belief and a fuller service, Wilfred regarded as little short of a positive duty. He desired, above all things, to protest against the vain and foolish cry after more knowledge, without respect to the work each man has to do and the material of which he is made. He thought both men and women ought to be better educated, but he wished them to have an education of purpose, directed to make them happy, satisfied, and effective in their individual circumstances.

It was not the good taste and varied and accurate knowledge evinced in Wilfred's writings which made them come home to the hearts of his readers, so much as the ready and frank appreciation of all human endeavor, and the deep sympathy with all human misery and weakness, which shone through them.

The quick way to popularity, however, is to mirror back to the age, in vivid coloring, its own thoughts in sharper outline, for distrust of novelty is one of the most marked national characteristics of our English people; but Wilfred Lane deserved, and ultimately won, a popularity which is of a slower growth. He did not simply reflect the thought of the day, but brought to it new thought and food. His theology, too, was anything but the theology of the so-called religious world, for he was as original as every man must be who has a strong conviction. His intense naturalism was fatal to all routine thinking. He put the standard of right and wrong, once and for all, inside every man instead of outside him. He felt that every one who wished his influence to be a marked one must work from within outwards, and bring to light his own individuality. He held that "whatever happens to a man is for the interest of the universe," and that "the whole contains nothing which is not for its advantage"—a theory which enabled him to bear, with cheerful composure, circumstances in his own life which would otherwise have been intolerable; and believing that the ruling part of man can make a material for itself out of that which opposes it, as fire lays hold of what falls into it, and rises higher by means of this very material, he persevered until he had made things his own; and what luxury is to those who enjoy pleasure, so to him was the doing of things comfortable to his nature.

He learnt to hold firmly to this and to be content with it.

At the same time Wilfred Lane was naturally inclined to regard the world in its divisions and subdivisions; and, under the aspect of individual cares and sorrows, was unduly impressed with the "night side of life." He had not yet fully realized life and light as synonymous, or, viewing existence in its entirety, seen the complete harmony of the whole.

CHAPTER XX.

"O Love, O fire! Once he drew
With one long kiss my whole soul thro'
My lips, as sunlight drinketh dew."
ALFRED TENNYSON.

As the hall-door of No. 10 Grosvenor Crescent was opened to Mr. Lane on the following afternoon, he was informed that Lady Harewood wished to see him alone in her boudoir, into which Watson ushered him with unusual formality, in evident obedience to some special command.

"I thought it was better to see you at once, Wilfred, as you requested me to do so," said his aunt, and she paused, thinking it would perhaps be better to allow her nephew to open the case himself, for she began to have a strong sense of the difficulty of her own position.

"After this long separation, which has tested Tiny's feeling for me, I hope you will consent to our marriage, and forgive me for coming to the point at once."

"My objections are only strengthened," said Lady Harewood, coldly.

"Surely you will not withhold your consent

now I am in a better position? Indeed I have always regarded it as promised in the event of Tiny's remaining attached to me on her return from Rome."

" I never made any promise of the kind."

" But you followed the plan I suggested," said Wilfred firmly, " and that condition was attached to it. I shall scarcely think that I am fairly dealt by if you still oppose our marriage. I am aware that Tiny might make a better match in a worldly sense, but you would find it impossible to confide her to any one who will love her more than I do, or seek her happiness more earnestly."

" I think your professions would be better proved by your yielding at once to the decision I feel bound to make for my daughter's good. Her father had the greatest possible objection to the marriages of cousins, and I am only acting in accordance with his wishes in opposing yours."

" That may be," he replied, with warmth, "but my uncle would have had some consideration for his child's affections. I am sure he would never have sacrificed Tiny's happiness to any theory."

Lady Harewood was conscious of the truth contained in Wilfred's answer, and, feeling somewhat beaten on this point, she resolved to start another.

" It is my consideration for Tiny which compels me to remind you, Wilfred, that she has not even had the test of six months' absence from you.

But I will not allow for one moment that, in following out what you are pleased to consider as
your suggestion, I am bound by any condition
you take the liberty of attaching to it."

"You surely remember that, after my conversation with Sir Anthony Claypole, the winter at
Rome was planned by me, because I felt unwilling
to urge that which you so strongly disapproved of,
without giving Tiny an opportunity of judging if
a marriage (unfortunately in opposition to your
wishes) was really essential to her happiness. Sir
Anthony saw me at your request, and when I told
him I should consider Tiny free to make any other
choice during her absence if you consented not to
oppose her ultimate decision, he said I could not
do more, and expressed himself perfectly satisfied
with my proposal."

"I had long thought of spending this winter
abroad, and it is quite absurd of you to lay such a
stress on your having talked it over with Sir
Anthony. I asked him to tell you how undesirable such a marriage was for Tiny, and what an
ungrateful return you would make for the kindness I have always shown you, if you persisted in
pressing the point, but Sir Anthony had no right
to answer for me; I should never authorize any
one to do so," and Lady Harewood grew quite
angry at the bare idea of such a thing.

"He did not answer for you, but he said he
thought you would see I had acted fairly in allow-

ing Tiny plenty of time to think over the matter, when away from my personal influence."

"I do not see that your mere separation has much to do with your influence, when you were constantly writing to Tiny, although you knew how I disapproved of your having any communication with each other. You appear to think that you have acted in a very magnanimous manner, Wilfred, but I confess I fail to see your conduct in that light."

Wilfred Lane felt thoroughly indignant, for Lady Harewood's tone was even more offensive than her words. With a great effort he controlled the angry remark which rose to his lips.

"I do not desire to appear magnanimous, but I have tried to act rightly," he replied, with dignity. "I felt you had every right to object to my proposal, and, still more, to think that my position had given me an undue advantage over Tiny; I was therefore ready to submit to a fair test, and Sir Anthony considered this was one."

"I am not bound to agree with even Sir Anthony Claypole's opinion," said Lady Harewood, sententiously, "and I repeat again that, keeping up by your constant letters the feelings you had already excited in Tiny's mind was not, in my opinion, giving her a proper opportunity of testing her feeling for you."

"Without seeing my letters," said Wilfred, firmly, "I submit that you are unable to judge me fairly."

"That in itself is a sufficient proof of their nature; Tiny would have shown me her *cousin's* letters," said his aunt, with an emphasis on the word cousin, and with a manner which, to Wilfred, was intolerable.

"I think not," he replied, gravely, "and I am not the person who is to be blamed for your daughter's want of confidence in you."

"Anyhow," said Lady Harewood, angrily, "I have quite made up my mind. I will never consent to your marriage with Tiny; and I tell you, Wilfred, plainly, that unless you are content to forfeit your position in my house, you must show some deference to my wishes. If you will promise me to forego this idea with regard to your cousin, I have sufficient reliance on your honor to allow you to visit here on your old footing; but if you persist in persuading Tiny to act in opposition to my commands, it will be my painful duty to deny you the house;" and opening the door which led into the drawing-room as she spoke, Lady Harewood put an end to any further conversation by joining her three daughters, who were talking to the two Miss Cunninghams and Colonel Fitzroy Somerset.

Wilfred followed his aunt, and when Tiny saw him she read in the troubled expression of his eyes something of the contest which was going on in his mind.

Sensitive to a degree which would be considered absurd by mere men of the world, the sensitive Wilfred was shrinking from the idea that, in order to secure his own happiness, he must bring dissension into his aunt's house, and that Tiny must defy her mother's commands. He did not feel, however, in the least disposed to relinquish Tiny, except at her own bidding; he had already sufficiently sacrificed himself and her by this weary separation, and his delicate sense of honor was shocked by Lady Harewood's manner of evading what appeared to him a tacit agreement.

Feeling disinclined to listen, in his present mood, to the "small talk" which was being carried on very vigorously by his cousins, after a few friendly words with Madeline, he asked Tiny to come down into the library, under the pretext of looking for a book he had lent her; an excuse which was made not to blind her mother, but to avoid exciting in the minds of her visitors any suspicion as to the real state of affairs.

When Wilfred closed the library-door, and found himself alone with Tiny, in spite of the unpleasant interview which had just taken place, he gave the answers he had promised to her letters, and did not attempt to control the passionate love, repressed during the weary weary weeks which had elapsed since last he stood alone in that room with her.

"My own darling," he said, as he kissed the

7

head nestling against his shoulder ; " if you really love me I will never give you up."

" Has mamma consented ? " asked his cousin, looking up eagerly into his face; " she was so unkind again last night about it, and said poor papa would never have agreed to it. I feel sure papa would, if he had ever promised to do so, and mamma ought to be bound by her word, now I have been to Rome."

" That is just what she disputes," said Wilfred with just indignation ; " your mother says that she never made any promise."

" But she did," persisted Tiny ; " I am sure Sir Anthony will think her very wicked for denying it, for he said if I went to Rome for the winter, mamma would be bound not to oppose us when I came back. What did she say to you, Wil ? "

Wilfred repeated his whole conversation with Lady Harewood; and when he came to the closing sentence, Tiny's indignation knew no bounds. She declared she would not remain at home, even if Wilfred agreed to desert her; in less than a month she would be of age, and nothing should induce her to live with her mother after such cruel conduct.

Tiny relieved her excitement by a good fit of crying, but Wilfred soothed her by the assurance of his love, and promised to induce Sir Anthony Claypole to mediate in the matter. He could not believe that Lady Harewood would refuse to listen to the representations of the old friend whose counsel she herself had sought, and if she did, Wilfred resolved on taking the matter into his own hands, and securing his own and Tiny's happiness with as little open defiance of the wishes of the family as was consistent with such a course of action. Kissing away her tears, he assured her that as her happiness was bound up in him, he would allow nothing in the world to separate them for long.

"You promised me that if I really loved you, nothing should part us, and I claim your promise now," pleaded Tiny, looking up into Wilfred's face in a way which caused his heart to beat quicker than usual, and sent his blood throbbing through every vein.

"No, my darling," he said, holding her still closer to him ; "I will never sacrifice such love as yours for any earthly consideration. I hardly know how to tear myself away from you now ; but if I don't go very quickly, I may lose the chance of seeing Sir Anthony to-day, and it is important to talk to him before your mother sees him, as she doubtless will to-morrow."

The number of times Wilfred said good-by would have been very inadmissible save in an affianced lover, but he had been parted from Tiny for so long, and had so completely restrained his deep, passionate love, that, now he allowed it expression, he found it difficult to control it at all.

Before he left, Tiny had taken from his watch-chain the signet ring, with the words "AD FINEM FIDELIS" engraved on the seal, which had belonged to his mother, and which Wilfred had often said should be his first present to his own wife.

As he placed it on Tiny's finger, she said to him, "Now you will always think of me as your own little wife, Wil ; for no horrid wedding breakfast and long white veil will ever make me feel more yours than I do at this very moment."

"God bless you, my darling one," said Wilfred. "I hold you to be my own true wife in the sight of God. I love you with all my heart, Tiny, and long for the hour when I shall call you mine in the eyes of the whole world."

CHAPTER XXI.

" Ah me ! For aught that ever I could read,
Could ever hear by tale or history,
The course of true love never did run smooth."
                                    SHAKESPEARE.

A HANSOM CAB was standing at the door of
Lady Harewood's house as Wilfred made his exit.
It had just deposited Sir Guy Fairfax, who had
heard at his club of the Harewoods' arrival from
Rome, and had come at once to pay his respects
to them.

Wilfred jumped into the Hansom, and induced
the driver to proceed as fast as possible to Hyde
Park Gardens, by the promise of an addition to
his ordinary fare. He could not refrain from smiling when he contrasted Sir Guy's probable haste
to the house in which he would see Tiny, and his
own despatch in leaving it, in order to promote
wishes which must put such an effectual barrier to
the hopes of his unfortunate but wealthy rival.

Sir Anthony Claypole was dressing for dinner
when Wilfred arrived, but he sent word that if Mr.
Lane would wait in the library, he would be with
him in a few minutes.

When he heard the state of the case, he felt very sorry for the young people, and was much perplexed as to the best way of helping them out of their difficulty. He thought Wilfred had every right to feel aggrieved by Lady Harewood's conduct, and could not wonder at his regarding it as a breach of faith. He and Tiny had made the sacrifice on the understanding that Lady Harewood would waive her objections, if Tiny was proof against the test Wilfred voluntarily imposed upon her.

Wilfred had rigidly refused himself much expression of his attachment during her absence, and had forced himself to write cold and cousinly letters ; but now, finding that Tiny's heart was so entirely his own, he determined to oppose Lady Harewood's refusal with the same persistency with which he had hitherto controlled himself.

"You must stay and dine with us, Lane ; we are quite alone this evening, and Lady Claypole will excuse your not being in evening dress," said Sir Anthony, after listening to Wilfred's account of his interview with Lady Harewood. "After dinner we will talk over the matter quietly, and if I can see my way to help you, you may rely on my doing so. I think you have behaved very well," added the kind old baronet, after a pause, laying his hand on Wilfred's shoulder, "and, by Jove, Lane, your aunt does not know a true man when she sees one ; and, as to her talk about good

matches," added the honest old baronet in a somewhat scornful tone, " she has never yet managed
to marry one of her daughters, with all her efforts,
and who knows if Fairfax would really come to
the point after all ? "

Now this was a view of the case for which
Wilfred was quite unprepared. He had an idea
that every man would come to the point with
Tiny, if he had only a chance of doing so. He
had even serious misgivings about Colonel Fitzroy
Somerset, who was as innocent of any matri-
monial intentions towards Tiny, or her sisters, as
any man who had never even seen them. But, in
this matter, Wilfred's love blinded him. His
usually calm judgment was unavailable in more
instances than one where Tiny was concerned.

The dinner passed off rather slowly and stiffly
as far as Wilfred was concerned, for though he
liked both Lady Claypole and her daughter, he
was anxious to talk alone with Sir Anthony over
his future prospects and his present position with
his aunt.

After the recent interview in the library, Wilfred
knew he could never resume a mere cousinly relationship with Tiny, and though he felt extremely
anxious to avoid an open rupture with her mother,
he had firmly resolved to submit to no further
barrier being placed between himself and that
little being who had so thoroughly twined herself
round his heart.

If Lady Harewood persisted in refusing her consent, Wilfred Lane felt he should defy her authority before very long.

As soon as the ladies had withdrawn, Sir Anthony took Wilfred into a small room, known by the household as " Sir Anthony's Study ; " Lady Claypole laughingly called it " The Tavern," for Sir Anthony used it as a smoking-room, and the apparent bookcase it contained, with its handsomely bound backs of volumes, disclosed, when opened by the pressure of a concealed spring at the side, sundry pipes, cigar boxes, tobacco jars, as well as some decanters containing French brandy and Scotch and Irish whiskey.

Not that Sir Anthony was addicted to drinking spirits, but he always smoked after dinner or before he went to bed, and liked to have something at hand, for the use of guests less abstemious than himself, without the trouble of ringing for his butler.

Wilfred only drank coffee when he smoked, but it must be confessed that he smoked a great deal. He had been obliged to do so for his health at first, and had learnt to look upon it as a pure enjoyment very soon. Besides this, he found that smoking soothed him, and often helped him to get through more work than he fancied he should have done without his pipe. In his excited nervous state, that evening, he was especially glad of

"Clouds of the peace-breathing Nicotiana,"

and, after an hour spent in Sir Anthony's sanctum,
he felt considerably calmer, and far better able to
take a hopeful view of his love affairs, though no
definite course of action had suggested itself.   Sir
Anthony had seen a great deal of his young friend
during the past winter, and had formed a very
high opinion of his character and intellectual
powers, which he thought would some day secure
Wilfred Lane a very high position.   He felt more
than ever surprised at Lady Harewood's persistent
refusal in the face of Tiny's evident attachment,
and shocked at her disinclination to keep a
promise which once made should have held sacred.

With Tiny's money, and Wilfred's present income, the young people would be far removed
from anything like poverty, and a better match, in
a worldly sense, was still only problematical.   Sir
Anthony Claypole really thought that if Lady
Harewood had any sense (and he always had
strong doubts upon that point), she ought to be
too thankful to secure such a husband for a
daughter whose wildness and waywardness might
very easily have taken a different and less satisfactory turn.

7*

CHAPTER XXII.

" Ah, what will the world say ? THE WORLD—therein lies
The question which, as it is uttered, implies
All that's fine or that's feeble in thought or intent."

OWEN MEREDITH.

SIR ANTHONY CLAYPOLE'S interview with
Lady Harewood· was not a pleasant one. He
gave her to understand in the most courteous
language that he considered she was not dealing
fairly by her nephew. Of course she inwardly resented this interference, and attempted to justify
her conduct by reference to the lamented Sir
Henry's opinions, whom she always quoted as an
authority when she desired to carry a point more
than usually unreasonable—a habit which suggested to his friends the very natural regret, that
she had not shown more consideration to her husband's wishes when he was able to define them in
person.

Sir Anthony Claypole apologized for any seeming presumption, but requested Lady Harewood
to remember that she had called forth his interference, in the first instance, by persuading him to
represent her feelings to Wilfred Lane. After
having induced that young man to propose what

appeared to him a fair test of Tiny's affection, he felt himself bound to remind Lady Harewood that the time had arrived when she was called upon to fulfil her part of the bargain, namely, to waive her objections to the marriage, and to show the consideration which, in Sir Anthony's opinion, her daughter's attachment for a man of Lane's high character deserved.

Lady Harewood made one excuse after another; first as to the time of her daughter's absence falling short of the prescribed six months; next as to Wilfred's letters, and so on through a host of difficulties, such as Tiny's age, her nephew's health, etc.; but she began to see that matters were assuming a serious aspect, and that a persistency in refusing her consent would be probably followed by an open rupture between herself and the Claypoles.

Sir Anthony did not even appear likely to remain neutral, but would probably support Wilfred and Tiny in their evident intention to disregard Lady Harewood's authority. Encouraged by this, she felt there was no saying what Tiny might not do, and it would be quite impossible to guess how the affair would end. Besides the feeling that she should not like to be openly defied by her daughter, the great dread of " what people would say " was always before her eyes.

The possibility of even a runaway match suggested itself!

Lady Harewood shuddered at the bare idea of such a scandal! She knew Tiny would not hesitate about it for a moment—in fact, such a step would have its attractions for this lawless little individual who was so Bohemian in her tastes; and although she had more confidence in her nephew, still there was a determination about him in their last interview which made Lady Harewood uneasy, for Wilfred had shown by his manner, even more plainly than by his words, that he considered his aunt had broken her promise, and had acted very badly towards both Tiny and himself.

He might not be capable of running away with his cousin in a base and underhand manner; but Lady Harewood thought him quite headstrong enough to marry Tiny in defiance of her wishes, especially as he declared that she had failed to keep her part of the engagement which he considered existed between them. If Sir Anthony meant to desert her, and give Wilfred and Tiny his support in this view of the matter, it was clear that something must be done. So Lady Harewood resolved on a compromise; and, knowing Wilfred's repugnance to set aside a parent's authority, she thought she would gain time by pledging her consent in a year, during which she determined to lose no opportunity of forwarding Sir Guy Fairfax's wishes.

So, after reiterating her previous objections, and bemoaning afresh over the loss of the lamented

Sir Henry's guidance at this critical moment, she promised her consent in a year's time ; meanwhile Wilfred should be allowed free access to the house, provided neither he nor Tiny paraded their feelings. Lady Harewood refused to acknowledge any " engagement," and stipulated that it should never be put forward as such.

It had taken such a long time to extract this concession, that Sir Anthony Claypole, not being an ardent young lover, but the sober. head of a well-organized household, felt disposed to rest satisfied with it. But he had no inclination again to undertake the task of representing Lady Harewood's sentiments even to her nephew, and thought it wiser under the circumstances to induce her to express them in writing.

So, before he left Grosvenor Crescent, he secured a promise that she would write to Wilfred, and that the year of probation should date from Tiny's birthday—the 1st of June.

And then Sir Anthony made his way down the staircase, resolving he would never again undertake the office which his friendship for Sir Henry Harewood and his interest in Wilfred Lane had in this instance induced him to accept ; and he muttered to himself as he walked to his club across the park, " women are queer cattle,"—a favorite reflection of his, but, happily for him, one which was rarely called forth in his own home.

The writing of the promised letter was ex-

tremely distasteful to Lady Harewood, yet she felt
there was no escape from it. Therefore she resolved to despatch it at once, and then intended to
give herself up to the headache which this disregard of her judgment and disrespect for her feelings would of course entail. So she began accordingly :—

" MY DEAR WILFRED,

" You are doubtless aware of Sir Anthony
Claypole's intercession on your behalf, and, as he
was such a respected friend of my dear and lamented husband, I feel anxious to listen to his
representations, although obliged to reserve my
own judgment. The responsibility, which rests
alone upon me, is very hard for any woman to
bear ; and is rendered doubly painful by the headstrong disposition of Tiny, which you have, in
my opinion, so inconsiderately fostered. Knowing my child's volatile and excitable nature as well
as I do, I cannot possibly consent, in such a
hurry, to your wishes, especially as I consider they
are most ill-judged. I do not believe that such a
marriage would eventually promote *your* happiness
any more than *hers*, and I fear you will live to regret your rashness if you follow your own desires
in defiance of the mature judgment to which it
would only be right for both of you at once to submit.

" However, as Sir Anthony urges it,—most re-

luctantly, and fearing that I am acting in a way
which your uncle would not have countenanced,
—I will consent to your marriage in a year from
this date, provided that you and Tiny, during that
time, appear before the world as cousins, and
never, by word or act, pretend that any kind of
engagement exists between you. Upon this condition, I will allow you to visit at my house as before.

" Your affectionate aunt,

"JANE HAREWOOD."

Before this letter reached Wilfred, he received a
visit from Sir Anthony, who warned him of its
contents, and advised him to avoid a family scandal by the acceptance of terms which appeared to
Wilfred exceedingly hard. Lady Harewood was,
in Sir Anthony's opinion, the most impracticable
woman he had ever met in his life ; and he considered any reasonable concession a great deal
more than could be expected from her. Anyhow,
he totally declined to undertake further negotia-
tions. Wilfred Lane must either accept what Sir
Anthony had, with so much difficulty, wrung from
her ladyship after three hours' talking, or else manage his affairs for himself.

So, when his aunt's epistle came, Wilfred felt
disposed to be thankful that, in the absence of
special directions from the " lamented Sir Henry,"
Lady Harewood had refrained from taking the

patriarch Jacob for her example, and commanded
her unlucky nephew to wait seven years for his
Rachel, and then married him to Charlotte instead.

A year was not so very long after all, and it was
not as if he were to be altogether shut out from
Tiny's society.   He was to have free access to
Grosvenor Crescent, and could see her every day.
Then, too, he would be able to save more money,
and when the time came for the marriage, would
be better able to make a comfortable home for his
wife.

After all, the waiting was harder for him than
for Tiny ; a reflection which again disposed Wilfred to a plan which not only avoided a family
quarrel, but (what appeared to him a far more
serious thing) an open and undutiful revolt on
Tiny's part against her mother's authority.

When Wilfred told Tiny that Lady Harewood
had been with difficulty persuaded to promise her
consent in a year's time, and of the condition she
imposed upon them meanwhile, that young lady
was by no means pleased.   And as to "their
friends not knowing they meant to marry each
other," she thought it "sheer nonsense," and held
up the little ring on her engaged finger most defi-
antly.

But after a conversation with Lady Harewood
matters were finally arranged.   Wilfred and Tiny
agreed to act in society scrupulously as cousins,
whatever they chose to consider between them-

selves ; and if, on the 1st of June in the following year, they still sought her consent to their marriage, Lady Harewood promised to withdraw all opposition, and to allow it to take place without further delay.

CHAPTER XXIII.

" The stronger will always rule, say some, with an air of confidence which is like a lawyer's flourish, forbidding exceptions, or additions. But what is strength? Is it blind wilfulness that sees no terror, no many-linked consequences, no bruises or wounds of those whose cords it tightens? Is it the narrowness of a brain that conceives no needs differing from its own, and looks to no results beyond the bargains of to-day; that tugs with emphasis for every small purpose, and thinks it weakness to exercise the sublime power of resolved renunciation? There is a sort of subjection which is the peculiar heritage of largeness and of love; and strength is often only another name for willing bondage to irremediable weakness."

GEORGE ELIOT.

FROM this moment Wilfred Lane never doubted Tiny's love. The proofs she had given of her attachment for him during her absence in Rome, and the difficulty he had to persuade her to submit to her mother's subsequent decision, made it impossible for him to suspect the depth of her affection, though her mother and her sisters evidently entertained a very different estimate of its value.

The year's waiting was very trying; for Wilfred Lane was a man who didn't care for the things which make the life of a bachelor very pleasant in London. He hated the butterfly existence which

so many are content to lead, and longed for the
pure and steady influence of a home he could call
his own, sweetened and sanctified by the presence
of the woman he could honor as well as love.

Wilfred had not been without temptations, and
to some of these he had succumbed ; but he had
never revelled in wickedness as many of his companions did, nor dissipated his affections by flirtations with every girl who came within reach of his
attractions. The only strong feeling he had ever
had, and to which, alas ! he had fatally yielded himself, was for a young and fascinating woman, whose
husband cruelly neglected her ; and into whose
society Wilfred had been most perilously thrown
at an age when he was most liable to fall a prey to
an influence exerted over him without intermission
or remorse.

But years had passed since he had broken this
spell, though the memory of it often haunted
him still. Once he spoke of it to Tiny, for the
remembrance sometimes made him feel unworthy
of the pure love which she lavished upon him.
To his surprise Tiny appeared to know a great
deal about it ; for, although Wilfred was aware
that the tale had come to Lady Harewood's ears,
he was hardly prepared to find it had been made
the subject of conversation with his young cousins.

Tiny, however, dismissed the unpleasant story
as a thing of the past, and Wilfred felt that this
early attachment had not really diminished his

power of loving this pure true-hearted girl who pledged herself to become his wife. Perhaps it even made him more capable of appreciating the feeling with which he regarded his cousin; he loved her with the same passionate intensity, but the passion was sanctified by the completeness of the union to which they both aspired.

Whenever he could leave his work, Wilfred made his way to Grosvenor Crescent, and shared with Tiny all the pleasures he allowed himself; and though they studiously avoided in society showing that a closer and stronger link than mere cousinhood bound them to each other, Tiny would often hold up her hand, when she saw Wilfred look at her, as if to assure him that the meaning of the ring she wore was never absent from her mind.

The pleasant readings, and the visits to the old haunts in search of favorite pictures, were all resumed, for Lady Harewood certainly kept to her promise of never attempting to control them.

" Society " troubled itself very little about the matter; people had always been accustomed to see Wilfred Lane with the Harewoods, and this constant attendance on Tiny excited little or no remark.

Of all the strange things of which this world is full, the unwarrantable power of *will* seems the strongest. Wilfred Lane's feeling for Tiny could scarcely be called simply love; it was the moral harnessing of a whole being to the will of another. As the action of the noblest horse is controlled by a slight leather, so is often the human heart by the will, which unconsciously (and in that often lies the secret of its power) directs it to the right and left at pleasure; and it is often the finer nature which is subjected to this magnetic power of will.

It was wonderful to see how completely Wilfred was swayed by Tiny. She was a wilful little maiden, with such coaxing winning ways, that she invariably did exactly what she liked with every one but her own mother.

For a long time Wilfred thought that all this would be altered when Tiny became his wife; but this was the license young ladies were allowed to indulge in towards their lovers; and as Tiny in general only required some little sacrifice of his personal wishes, he was ready enough to yield; but occasionally a sense of disappointment flitted across his mind.

There were also several subjects of dispute in the home circle. Tiny's determination to absent herself from the balls and parties, at which she knew Wilfred would not appear, gave her mother great displeasure.

These were the very places to which Lady Harewood was most anxious to take her, especially when there was the remotest chance of meeting Sir Guy Fairfax, who was kept in blissful ignorance of the understanding, or, as Tiny would have it, of the *engagement* between herself and her cousin.

Lady Harewood appealed to Wilfred; but as Tiny made her health a plea for not going into hot and crowded rooms, he declined to interfere in the matter.

Sir Guy Fairfax, however, had other opportunities given him, of which he took every advantage, and at last Wilfred could not refrain from feeling sorry for the young man; for it appeared unfair of his aunt to encourage him so openly, when she knew the state of Tiny's mind precluded all hope of the result for which Fairfax was now so earnestly and honestly striving.

Concealment and secrets of all kinds were foreign to Wilfred's nature; knowing that both he and Tiny regarded themselves as pledged to each other, Wilfred often felt he acted dishonorably in even consenting to pass as her mere cousin.

The season, at last, came to an end. The last dinner engagement had been kept; the last ball had afforded the dancers, for the first time, sufficient space to enjoy themselves; the opera was about to commence its series of " cheap nights," and the West End of London was beginning to look deserted.

Tiny and Wilfred were looking forward to a

delightful expedition, which had been planned especially for their benefit by the thoughtful kindness of the good-natured Sir Anthony Claypole, who had invited the Harewoods to go with him for a cruise, in his yacht, as soon as Wilfred Lane could get leave of absence from the War Office.

CHAPTER XXIV.

"No, there's nothing half so sweet in life
As love's young dream."
MOORE'S IRISH MELODIES.

ONE Saturday afternoon in August, Lady Harewood, Madeline, and Tiny met Wilfred at the London Bridge station, and travelled together to Gravesend.

Sir Anthony, at first, proposed to start from Southampton, but had ordered his yacht round to Gravesend, out of deference to Lady Harewood, who hated railway travelling as heartily as she considered it ladylike to hate anything.

Sir Anthony and Miss Claypole awaited their friends' arrival on board the Highflyer, where they found an excellent dinner ready for them, during which Sir Anthony advised his guests to drink plenty of champagne, recommending it as the best possible thing to enable them to maintain their reputation as good sailors.

After dinner every one came on deck, and soon the yacht gave sundry signs of "getting under weigh," and, before long, she was moving slowly down the Thames. Tiny showed a singular inclination to improve her geographical knowledge, and Wilfred found plenty of occupation in telling her the names of the different places they passed on each side of the river. There was a splendid moon that night, and long after Lady Harewood retired, her daughters and Miss Claypole remained on deck with the two gentlemen, enjoying the calm beauty of the evening, and rejoicing in the thought of the freedom which would be theirs for the next four weeks.

London, with its close stifling atmosphere, and its still more stifling conventionality, was surely, if slowly, being left behind, and now that Lady Harewood—the only element which reminded them of that oppressive atmosphere—was safely shut up in her cabin, a more congenial party could hardly have been found.

The time slipped away so pleasantly, that it was nearly twelve o'clock before even Madeline suggested that they ought to think of following her mother's example; but they were all so loth to go below, that they agreed to cast lots as to who should repeat a favorite poem, and sing a song in order to gain a few more moments' enjoyment of the exquisite starlight night.

Strangely enough, and to the great satisfaction of the ladies, the lots fell upon the two gentle-men; Sir Anthony caused considerable merriment by immediately serenading London in Lord Byron's words, " Isle of beauty, fare thee well," to a

8

new and original melody ; after which Wilfred appropriately repeated Heine's delightful lines on the wisdom of the stars :

> " The flowerets sweet are crushed by the feet,
>   Fall soon, and perish despairing ;
> One passes by, and they must die,
>   The modest as well as the daring.
>
> The pearls all sleep in the caves of the deep,
>   Where one finds them, despite wind and weather ;
> A hole is soon bored, and they're strung on a cord,
>   And there fast yoked together.
>
> The stars are more wise, and keep in the skies,
>   And hold the earth at a distance ;
> They shed their light in the heavens so bright,
>   In safe and endless existence."

With many lingering good-nights and regrets the first happy evening of the yachting excursion came to an end, the deck was deserted, and the friends separated for the night.

When the morning dawned, every one on board the Highflyer realized the fact that they were " at sea ; " for the wind had risen during the night, and the little yacht was tossing and dancing about off the South Foreland in anything but a pleasant manner, and beating to windward in a way enough to discomfort any ordinary landsman. The ladies were far too sick and sorry to leave their berths ; and though Wilfred just managed to get on deck, and was trying to put a good face on the matter, any ardor for salt water, with which he had started, seemed permanently cooled; and he was forced to confess to himself that he was glad there was no one to witness his discomfiture, or notice the pertinacity with which he held on to the side of the vessel.

Even Sir Anthony Claypole's affection for the sea was of the most subdued and sober description; and his position as host made him feel somewhat guilty of the miseries old Father Neptune was inflicting on his confiding guests.

The weather continued, in nautical language, so exceedingly "foul," and the ladies so hopelessly sick, that the Highflyer put back into the first convenient harbor. An hour after she was fairly anchored in quiet waters, one pale face after another appeared on deck, until the whole party reassembled, but in very different spirits to those in which they had separated the night before.

A walk on shore, however, revived those who felt strong enough to take it; and some cold chicken and champagne, the first food any of them had tasted that day, completed the cure.

Sir Anthony allowed his friends to retire to rest in the happy belief that they should remain all night in the harbor; but as the wind had changed at sunset, he determined to put out to sea, for the captain thought they could manage to reach Southampton soon after daybreak. The whole party slept so soundly that they were unconscious

of the movement of the vessel, and to their delight
and surprise they breakfasted the next morning in
Southampton waters.

Finding he had such a sorry set of sailors for his
guests, and that their notion of yachting was to
hasten on shore at the first opportunity, Sir
Anthony Claypole resolved to sacrifice his own
intentions of a more extended cruise; and, to
make the month's holiday as enjoyable as he
could, he determined to hover between Cowes,
Ryde, and Freshwater, and to explore the interior
of the island, using the yacht chiefly as a mov-
able sleeping-place.

Tiny was in the wildest spirits; she and Wilfred
delighted in the most perfect freedom, for there
was no Sir Guy Fairfax or "society" at hand to
oblige them to keep forever on their guard lest
they should break the compact to which Lady
Harewood compelled such a rigid outward adherence.

During the last week of their stay at Cowes, the
Ariel, General Hallyburton's yacht, anchored in
the night next to the Highflyer.

The General was an old friend of Sir Anthony's,
and shortly after breakfast the Ariel's boat pulled
alongside, and he came on board, accompanied by
his yachting companion, Captain Foy.

When Tiny saw Captain Foy she was so completely taken by surprise, that Wilfred's attention
was attracted by her nervousness and evident want

of ease. Captain Foy was, of course, perfectly self-possessed ; he knew that Lady Harewood and her daughters were cruising in the Highflyer : and had quite recovered from the fears which induced him to avoid Tiny immediately after the vehement Windsor flirtation, and finding a long sail with General Hallyburton somewhat dull, he sighed for the variety which the proximity of the Harewoods seemed likely to afford.

So, after the first greetings were over, he warmly seconded a proposed excursion to the back of the island, where they all had mutual friends, on whose hospitality they contemplated throwing themselves for a few hours during the middle of that day.

This was no sooner planned than put into execution, and the whole party landed before eleven o'clock at the point to which the steward had already been despatched to meet them with carriages for the day's expedition.

Somehow or other Tiny took her place in the carriage containing Lady Harewood and Sir Anthony, and Captain Foy quickly availed himself of the fourth seat, compelling Wilfred, to his great disgust, to join Miss Claypole, Madeline, and General Hallyburton. Later on in the day, as they all walked on the Downs at Freshwater, Wilfred told Tiny they must manage better in going back, but strange to say she did not appear half so eager about it ; and while final arrange-

ments were being made with the hostlers who had
taken charge of the horses, the ladies settled themselves in their different places for the homeward
drive, and returned as they came, with the exception of Sir Anthony and his daughter, who
changed places at the last moment, to enable the
former to drive back in the same carriage with
General Hallyburton. Before the friends parted,
Sir Anthony promised, if the wind proved fair, to
bring his guests the following day on board the
Ariel, for a sail as far as the Needles.

The day's expedition certainly did not seem so
successful to Wilfred Lane as it promised to be
when they all left the yacht that morning ; and
Tiny apparently was indulging in the same reflection. Anyhow she was clearly out of spirits, and
unusually thoughtful and silent.

After dinner every one came on deck ; the
evening was peculiarly still and lovely, and the
new moon exquisitely beautiful.

Talking over the events of the day, Lady Harewood expressed her astonishment at finding
Captain Foy had never been engaged to Miss
Peel, notwithstanding the rumors they had heard to
that effect, during the season previous to their visit
to Rome. Tiny's face flushed as her mother spoke ;
rising from her seat, she complained of being chilly,
and began to walk up and down the deck.

In a few minutes Wilfred joined her, but neither
of them seemed inclined to talk.

Tiny had already begun to be conscious of a return of the old Windsor feeling, and, in spite of herself, she was engrossed in wondering over the state of Captain Foy's mind. Perhaps, after all, thought Tiny, he had mistaken the way in which she regarded him ; and his apparent sentiment for Miss Peel was a mere screen for the disappointment he experienced when he thought he had failed to reach her heart. She recalled many little speeches she had made, which might easily have been misinterpreted ; and ended by thinking that, but for these, Captain Foy would long ago have declared his love. Of course he was too proud and sensitive to risk a proposal, when she always made a point of turning his attempts at tenderness into ridicule, or else appeared annoyed and offended by the very words she longed to hear from his lips !

Wilfred and Tiny had ceased to pace the deck, and were now leaning over the side of the yacht. The foolish little maiden had just arrived at the conclusion that she had given Captain Foy a life-long sorrow as well as herself, and that she was alone to blame for their mutual disappointment, when Wilfred took her hand and pointed to the beautiful reflection of the moon, and the sparkling ripples of the water.

For the first time Tiny impatiently repulsed his affection.

" I am so tired to-night," she said, somewhat

peevishly, drawing away her hand. "I wish you would go and talk to the others; my head aches, and I want to be quiet."

Wilfred left her, and, asking leave to light his cigar, sat down by Madeline.

For some time he smoked in silence, wondering over Tiny's pale face and irritable manner. He felt certain something had moved her deeply, and yet he could not imagine what it was, for he never dreamt that day of connecting Tiny's change of mood with Captain Foy's presence or absence.

Very shortly there was a general move, and Tiny, instead of staying behind as she was accustomed to do, for a few minutes' talk with Wilfred, went below with the others, only wishing him and Sir Anthony, who was also smoking, a careless good-night as she passed them.

The next day's sail opened Wilfred's eyes to one fact. He could not tell what had gone before, but certainly, at the present moment, Captain Foy paid Tiny very marked attention, and she betrayed a greater interest in him than Wilfred thought her relation with himself and acquaintance with Foy at all warranted.

This went on for days; for if General Hallyburton and his guests were not on board the Highflyer, Sir Anthony and his party sailed in the Ariel, or they made some inland excursion together. All this time Tiny successfully eluded being alone with Wilfred without appearing to do so intentionally.

One bright morning, when Wilfred came on deck, he could not suppress a feeling of satisfaction on discovering that the Ariel had forsaken her moorings. He knew by this that General Hally-burton had carried his threat into execution, and sailed at daybreak for Cherbourg.

Before Foy could return the Highflyer would have left for Dartmouth, according to the arrange-ment of the previous night. For once Wilfred blessed Lady Harewood for carrying her point about seeing the Devonshire coast, which she had done rather in opposition to the rest of the party, who were evidently in favor of still coasting round the Isle of Wight.

Tiny's apparent indifference when Sir Anthony announced at breakfast the departure of his friends somewhat re-assured Wilfred, who straightway accused himself of mean and jealous feelings, unworthy of himself and of his love and devotion for Tiny.

It had been agreed the day before that the two yachts should sail together to Ryde, unless the Cherbourg plan came off, which Captain Foy heartily hoped it would not. So the Highflyer was already under weigh before breakfast was fin-ished, and a fair wind soon brought her within a convenient landing distance from the pier.

Just as they were preparing to leave the yacht,

8*

Tiny excused herself from going on shore, on the plea of a headache, and when Wilfred offered to stay with her, she for once heartily echoed her mother's objection, and declined his proposal on the ground that she would be more likely to get better if left quite alone.

So they started without her; but to Wilfred the day was thoroughly spoilt. He had looked forward to it so eagerly, directly he found the Ariel had set sail for Cherbourg, hoping that the happy freedom of the first fortnight would return.

There were atmospheric clouds, too, about, which threatened to damp their pleasure after another fashion, and the party returned to the yacht much sooner than they had intended.

When Wilfred saw Tiny he felt certain that she had been crying.

At dinner, however, she seemed in her usual spirits, and lingered on deck as before, when her mother and Madeline retired.

Sir Anthony and his daughter were talking over some second post letters which had only just been brought on board, and Wilfred took this opportunity to ask Tiny suddenly, as he drew her hand within his arm for a walk up and down the deck, what had made her look so unhappy?

The question seemed to startle her; acting on the impulse of the moment, as she generally did, Tiny told Wilfred the whole story about Captain Foy; confided to him her feelings during the winter spent at Windsor, and her subsequent doubts and disappointment.

She was so perfectly engrossed with her own thoughts that she was utterly unconscious of the effect of her disclosure upon her cousin. But when Wilfred asked her if Captain Foy had *now* told her that he loved her, his voice was so unlike his own that Tiny looked up in his face, and the pain she read in it awoke within her a sudden sense of the sorrow she had inflicted upon him.

" Oh, Wil," she cried, " I know I have done what is wrong. I ought not to have concealed this from you ; many many times I have longed to tell you, but the words have died on my lips. I could not bear that any one should know about it. And there *is* nothing to know," she added, passionately, " for he has never said that he loved me."

" There is something for *me* to know, Tiny," he replied, his voice trembling with suppressed emotion. " If you have such a feeling for this man, how can you say you love me ? "

" I do love you, Wilfred ; but it is not exactly the same. I never could care for two people in the same way. Don't blame me," she said, clinging with both hands round his arm, and looking up eagerly into his eyes, " don't blame me for not having told you. I thought I never should see him any more, and that he would marry Miss Peel. And I have felt so happy in loving you—"

She paused as if she had not finished her sentence.

"Until you saw him again," said Wilfred, calmly.

Tiny burst into tears.

They were standing on the side of the vessel, looking towards Ryde; Sir Anthony and his daughter had already gone below, and they had the whole deck to themselves.

Presently Tiny looked up.

"You are not angry with me, Wil, darling? I can't help it; you see it was before I cared for you. I did not know how weak I was till I saw him again, but it will be all right soon," she added, in a firmer tone.

"It can't be all right, Tiny, if you feel this now. But, thank God," he exclaimed, with great effort controlling his own feeling, "it has come in time. You are still free. Your mother was right, after all," he added, with a sigh.

"But you will not leave me, Wil? He has never said he loved me, and I don't believe he does. Don't leave me, Wilfred," she continued vehemently, "now that I feel as if I wanted you more than ever."

Before Wilfred could reply he became conscious of the presence of a third person. Madeline came with a message from her mother, who considered it unwise for Tiny to stay so late on deck after her indisposition; and whilst she waited for her sister,

Tiny had only just time to whisper, " Don't say a word till I speak to you to-morrow, Wil, darling," and, with the most affectionate look she had given him since the Ariel came into Cowes, she disappeared down the cabin stairs.

Wilfred Lane felt bewildered. He had never thought it possible that Tiny would prove faithless to him, nor imagined her capable of such a concealment ; nor had he ever doubted that she had given him her first and best affection. It was a new revelation, and one which scattered all his previous belief in Tiny's disposition and character.

He paced up and down the deck hour after hour, thinking over what he had heard that night ; scarcely able to realize that Tiny had ever cared for any one but himself. When he recalled her tenderness to him, and the letters she had written from Rome, it was impossible to believe she had ever loved another.

Since the day Tiny had worn his mother's ring Wilfred had regarded their union as indissoluble, in spite of Lady Harewood's opposition. Tiny's unexpected confession respecting a love which was not the growth of to-day, but which had existed even before she consented to be his wife, and which it seemed to him she had strangely nourished ever since, absolutely stunned him.

His thoughts beyond this took no definite shape ; he never attempted to consider how to act with regard to their present relative position, or Captain

Foy's ultimate intentions towards Tiny. He had to grow familiar with one great fact, which stood out clear at last; his belief in Tiny's first love was a delusion. She had deceived him, and he had deceived himself.

He could think no more; but as he rested his head against his hands, which were clasped round a rope above him, the pain of parting at Folkestone, and the desolateness of the winter which followed while Tiny was in Rome, seemed nothing to his present misery.

Presently he was startled by a hand laid on his shoulder, and, turning round, he saw Sir Anthony, who exclaimed, "Why, Lane, whatever are you doing? It is just five o'clock, and you have never been to roost."

Wilfred stammered out as an excuse that he had been restless; that, as he shared Sir Anthony's cabin, he feared to disturb him, and therefore had remained on deck.

"My head aches, too," he added, "and I thought the cool air would do me good, but I'll go and turn in now, and perhaps I shall sleep it off." And Wilfred moved away, glad to escape any further questioning.

CHAPTER XXV.

"Alas! how easily things go wrong,
A sigh too much—or a kiss too long—
And there comes a shower and a driving rain,
And life is never the same again.

Alas! how hardly things go right,
'Tis hard to watch through the summer night,
For the kiss will come, and the sigh will stay,
And the summer night is a winter day."
                                        GEORGE MACDONALD.

"People are always talking of perseverance, courage, and fortitude; but patience is the finest and worthiest part of fortitude—and
the rarest too."

                                        JOHN RUSKIN.

AT breakfast Wilfred's countenance bore but
little trace of the suffering he had gone through
during the night. Had any one noticed him particularly, they would have remarked he was more
silent than usual; but as he was never a great
talker, his silence was unobserved on this occasion.

Tiny, however, was in the best of spirits, and
surprised everybody by her outbursts of fun and
merriment. It seemed impossible that beneath
this joyous exterior she could be enduring much

mental pain, and Wilfred began to think he had exaggerated the matter in his own mind. But then again came the recollection that for all these months Tiny, while professing to treat him with entire frankness, had concealed from him the very fact that she had ever cared for any man except himself, and Wilfred was exceedingly troubled as he thought of this.

By eleven o'clock the yacht was under weigh, and a smart steady wind bore her on towards Portland. As far as outward circumstances went, this was one of the pleasantest sails they had yet made, but everything seemed changed to Wilfred. All the joy and brightness he had known during the last few weeks was gone. There was a dull leaden pain in his heart, and a dark though undefined dread overclouded the future which but yesterday seemed charged with happiness.

The first moment that he was alone with Tiny she slipped her hand in his, and said in her gentlest voice, " Wilfred, I am so sorry I· made you unhappy last night; I should have told you ages ago, but for this ; and now I have spoken, I dare say you have lost all confidence in me ? "

" No, Tiny ; but you have surprised me so much that I don't know what to think, except that you must be free, after what you have told me. I don't want to blame you, darling, but you never should have hidden it from me."

" I was afraid to tell you, Wilfred, because I

thought how it would be.   You don't love me any
longer, I see," and Tiny looked into his eyes with
an eager longing gaze.

"Yes, Tiny, I do love you—it would seem as
easy to root out my heart itself as to root out the
love it holds for you.   I should not feel the misery
I do, in the thought that I have not the power to
make you happy, if I did not love you."

"But you do make me happy," she answered
impulsively.   "I have been happier and better
ever since you loved me, and till this week I never
thought that other feeling would come back."

"Then your feeling for this man has come back
to you?" asked Wilfred, in a tone which betrayed
his suffering.

"Not exactly come back to me," she answered
thoughtfully.   "I don't know how it is, but it
seems impossible to shake off altogether the remembrance of that winter at Windsor."

Tiny's hand with Wilfred's ring on it was in his
own as she spoke; as she finished her sentence,
he said quietly, "Let me put this back on my
chain, Tiny; you must indeed be free; there
could be no happiness for either of us in this now.
We have made a mistake, but it is not yet too late
for you."

"Oh, Wil; how can you be so cruel?   I wish
I had never told you.   I do not seem able to
make you understand me.   It is not that I love
Captain Foy; it was only the remembrance of the

past which upset me while he was here. You
know what a strange mind I have, and sometimes
I think if I could only tell whether he loved me or
not I should feel quite content; but now I cannot
help dwelling on it, and all the little things he used
to say. It was very wicked of him," said Tiny,
pensively, " to seem so miserable whenever I would
not walk or ride with him, if he did not really care
for me. What did he mean by it, Wilfred ? "

" How can I tell you, Tiny ? " he answered, betraying for the first time an impatience it was hard
to restrain as his cousin's selfishness became too
palpable for even his deep love to remain blind to
it any longer ; " I know so little of this man, and
love you so much, that I am no judge. I can
scarcely even tell what is best for us ; but you
must be quite free. Give me back the ring, Tiny ;
now I know of your feeling for Captain Foy I dare
not—will not claim your sweet promise to be my
wife."

" That is just what I feared "—and Tiny grew
quite pale and shook with her little piteous sobbing—" and that is why I never told you before ;
it is cruel, Wilfred, of you to forsake me now, just
when I want you more than ever."

" I don't forsake you, child," cried Wilfred ;
" God knows I want your happiness before my
own ! I love you well enough to wish to see you
happy in your own way ; but I never thought that
happiness would be apart from mine."

" But it is not, Wil ; I never could do without you ; have patience with me," pleaded Tiny. " I don't know what brought up this old feeling, and I was very foolish to tell you of it last night. Oh, Wil, it seems so cruel to think you will love. me less now. I will not give you back my ring," she added with a vehemence which startled Wilfred ; " I could not do without you ! "

Neither of them spoke for a few minutes, until Tiny said in a quiet tone, " I don't think, Wilfred, men ever do understand women. I thought you would ; but you don't seem in the least to know what I really feel."

" Tiny, you cannot love me and Captain Foy ; the thing is impossible. One of us must give place to the other."

" But he has never said he loved me," persisted Tiny.

" But *you* love him," replied Wilfred, as if the very words scorched him.

" No, I don't," Tiny answered, as if she had that very moment arrived at that conclusion. " I have a strange interest in him ; whatever happens I shall have that all my life. He was the first to awaken in me any real feeling, and that is what you, as a man, cannot understand. No girl can ever be quite the same again."

" You ought to have told me of this before, Tiny, and not have allowed me to believe that my love first called forth yours. And you

seemed ready enough to give it when I asked
it from you."

"If you had come to me as a stranger, Wil, it
would have been very different; but my affection for you as a cousin led me on step by step,
until unconsciously you crept into my heart.
You came to me as the best and highest influence
I ever had in my life. Don't forsake me, Wil;
I think I should grow wicked if you left me now.
Why should you not love me all the same? I
am the same as I was yesterday; the only difference is that you know more of me than you did.
It ought to show you," said Tiny, in a pleading
voice, and looking up at him with her old passionate expression, "how much I love you and have
trusted you."

Wilfred Lane did not quite see this, but he felt
the power of Tiny's fascination. Perhaps she
was right, and that he could not enter into a girl's
inmost heart. It did not seem, however, as if
Captain Foy loved Tiny; it was more than
probable that he had only trifled with her after
the fashion of men of his kind.

And then, too, Tiny evidently depended on him
for support; she had even pleaded for his love;
how could he be so base and cruel as to desert her
in such need? Had everything in his own life
been so clear and blameless that he should claim
as his lawful due the first undivided affection
of this girl, and because he found that another

man had once had power to move her, was it generous of him to say " I also will give you up"? It would be quite another thing if Captain Foy had claimed the love he had awakened; then Wilfred's path would have been very clear; he must have accepted his own misery at once, and perhaps in time his heart might have ached less when he remembered that each pang it suffered secured his darling's happiness.

To leave her now, was only to make her position more difficult. If Captain Foy really loved her, he would return and say so, for, as he had no idea of Tiny's engagement,—there was nothing to prevent his coming forward.

But Wilfred could not help thinking Captain Foy never intended to come forward. He therefore resolved to do as Tiny asked him; she might keep his ring, but he would consider her free.

He would do still more. As far as he could compass it, she should have fair play. His love for Tiny was deep enough to enable him to sacrifice himself.

.   .   .   .

After a day at Portland, the Highflyer cruised round the Devonshire coast for a week. The morning after she reached Plymouth, Sir Anthony received a letter from his wife, telling him that she was glad his month's yachting had nearly come to an end, for she had been very sick, and during the last few days had been obliged to call in the family physician. As Sir Anthony believed that more people "died of the doctor" than "by the visitation of God," this information naturally made him anxious; so it was settled that Margaret should go to London by train, and rejoin her mother at once, while her father returned with the rest of the party, viâ Southampton, for which place they set sail the same evening.

It was naturally a matter of constant pain to Wilfred to see how completely all Tiny's thoughts were taken up in the feeling which she had expended on one who was in his opinion utterly unworthy of them. And sometimes it was almost more than he could bear to listen to her continual perplexities about the meaning of some trivial circumstance, which had been treasured up in her mind as something of great consequence—for, now that the ice was broken, Tiny did not scruple to confide to Wilfred, with a frankness which utterly amazed him, every little incident which happened that winter, including even the secret meetings in the shrubberies, and Captain Foy's parting kiss.

Few men would have borne this with such perfect self-command; but Wilfred seldom betrayed to Tiny the pain she inflicted upon him. His love for her was of too deep and unselfish a nature to admit of his shrinking from any suffering which might give his darling even an instant's relief.

Sometimes Wilfred Lane thought that the very repression of Tiny's past feeling had tended to foster it; at any rate he hoped that the complete confidence which now existed between them would tend to increase her trust in him. He could not doubt that she had by degrees given him a far stronger affection than mere cousinship warranted, and he earnestly prayed for that day to come when Tiny's little mind would cease to be disquieted at all about this Captain Foy. Her perfect openness with him certainly seemed a rivet in the chain which bound them together, and, resting content with this reflection, Wilfred shut his eyes to any future sorrow he might be heaping up for himself.

CHAPTER XXVI.

"Places are too much
Or else too little, for immortal man;
Too little, when love's May o'ergrows the ground,
Too much, when that luxuriant robe of green
Is rustling to our ankles in dead leaves.
'Tis only good to be or here or there,
Because we had a dream on such a stone,
Or this or that,—but, once being wholly waked
And come back to the stone without the dream,
We trip upon't, alas, and hurt ourselves;
Or else it falls on us and grinds us flat,
The heaviest gravestone on this burying earth."

MRS. BARRETT BROWNING.

WEEK after week flew by, but Captain Foy never made his appearance in Grosvenor Crescent. The Harewoods knew he had not returned in the Ariel to Cowes, for they had seen General Hallyburton again, at the Claypoles', who told them that his guest had deserted him at Cherbourg, having met a friend who persuaded him to join in a walking tour through Normandy.

Lady Claypole had quite recovered from her indisposition, and all the Harewoods and Wilfred Lane were dining at Hyde Park Gardens in order to talk over the "cruise in the Highflyer," when

General Hallyburton happened to look in for a quiet smoke with his friend in " the tavern," and was at once brought upstairs into the drawing-room, as a person immediately concerned with the cruise in question. So he contributed his share to the evening's entertainment, in which was included much information about Captain Foy.

But this was soon after their return from the yacht. Since then Tiny had heard from the Howards that Captain Foy was in town and had been there on the previous Sunday. So it became evident that he was least in no hurry to call on the Harewoods.

Gradually Tiny's mind seemed to settle down; her speculations respecting Captain Foy's past, present, and future intentions became less frequent, and her anxiety to hear about him perceptibly diminished. Wilfred Lane at last fancied himself in sight of the " promised land" which he had striven so hard to win, and he really thought the time was not far distant when his darling's undivided affection would be his own.

Towards the end of October the Harewoods again left town, and were scattered about the country, visiting different friends.

One of the last visits Madeline and Tiny intended to pay together was to The Cedars. Mrs. Wroughton's former kindness to Tiny made it quite impossible for her to go on inventing excuses, whenever an invitation to spend a few days

9

at Windsor arrived. Her sisters had already remarked upon former evasions, and Charlotte often called Tiny very ungrateful for not caring to go to her old friends. So, in spite of Tiny's unwillingness, a visit was at last arranged. She and Madeline engaged to spend a week at The Cedars, where Lady Harewood and Charlotte were to join them for a few days, after which they were all to return to London together.

As the carriage which had been sent to meet them at the Windsor station drove rapidly into the park gates, there was a keen and frosty feeling in the air, which reminded Tiny vividly of the visit she seemed destined never to forget. Her heart beat with a thousand recollections which instantly crowded upon her, and she almost felt as if she could not bear to see the place which was full of such sweetly bitter memories. As she turned her face away from the path which led down to the lake, where she and Captain Foy used to go and feed the lonely black swan who had lost his mate, her eye caught the curling blue smoke of Miss Foy's chimneys, above the trees which concealed her cottage at the further end of the park. Tiny could almost fancy that, if she looked long enough, she should see the figure of Captain Foy treading its way through the clump of trees which led by the shrubbery to the rose garden, which had often served as their trysting-place.

Several times Madeline spoke to her; but Tiny

was so wrapped up in her own thoughts that she never even heard her sister, until she took hold of her arm, exclaiming—

"Whatever are you thinking of, Tiny? I have spoken twice, and you don't answer me."

"I was thinking"—began Tiny, and she paused for a moment, and then continued hastily—"I don't know what I was thinking of; but I know I hate talking in a close carriage, and my head aches so dreadfully that I wish I might go to bed when we get in."

There was no time for further speech or reflection, for the carriage had already reached the door, and Mrs. Wroughton came out to welcome her guests in the hall—a good old fashion which she never neglected. Five o'clock tea was going on in the library, and the first person Tiny saw, as she entered, was Miss Foy, who had come up early to dine and sleep at The Cedars, for her delicate state of health still obliged her to avoid the night air.

There were several other people in the room, among them Admiral Merryweather, Colonel and Mrs. Ashburton, and Mr. Philpots, the incumbent of the small church which the Wroughtons attended, when they had no visitors who wished to hear the music at St. George's Chapel, Windsor.

As Tiny knew nearly all Mrs. Wroughton's county friends, much shaking of hands ensued, and Madeline was introduced to Mr. Philpots.

A general re-distribution of seats taking place,

Tiny went over to the sofa on which Miss Foy was sitting, and there installed herself.

When Miss Foy had discussed the journey the Miss Harewoods had just made, the disagreeables attendant on railway travelling in general, and the excellence of the Windsor line in particular, Tiny turned the conversation upon the weather, hoping, by sundry comparisons between this winter, last winter, and the winter before that, to carry back the listener's mind to the time of her nephew's visit, knowing that when she was reminded of Captain Foy's existence she would be sure to mention him. Tiny felt shy about speaking first herself. Conscious of her own intense longing to hear of him, she did not even dare to make inquiries which would have simply appeared to his aunt natural and polite.

Her little stratagem had its desired effect. As soon as Miss Foy recalled that peculiarly severe winter, and her consequent confinement to her room, she thought how her good Philip had refused to leave her, and how thankful she then was that The Cedars and its pleasant occupants, including the Harewood family, afforded him an occasional solace, during the days when she was too ill to see him at all.

"Speaking of that winter reminds me of Philip," she said; "you remember him, I think, for you were kind enough to help my friends here to entertain the dear fellow. I never shall forget how

good he was," continued the old lady, gratefully.
" Nothing would induce him to leave me till the
spring, when his sister returned from abroad, and
I am sure it must have been very dull work to stay
with a wheezing old aunt like me."

" I hope you are stronger now," said Tiny,
rather hypocritically, for she could not resist wishing in her heart that Miss Foy was ill again, and
once more enjoying her nephew's solicitude. " I
remember how anxious Captain Foy was about
you, but he told us when we met him in the Isle
of Wight that you were much better."

" Yes, thank you, I am really stronger, I believe ;
so I tell Philip he has lost his chance of coming
into possession of the Wilderness soon enough for
it to be of any use to him. Such a small place,"
she added, smiling, " will scarcely do for Lady
Susan, though it would have suited Philip very
well as a bachelor."

Tiny could not understand this reference to
" Lady Susan."

Lady Susan *who?* she felt inclined to say
eagerly ; and she thought it *so* provoking of people to talk in such a way. She was quite angry
with Miss Foy for supposing that she must be acquainted with every circumstance connected with
her nephew's future requirements, and her heart
beat so violently that she feared Miss Foy would
hear it if she did not speak. Controlling herself
with a great effort, she remarked that " the Wil-

derness was one of the prettiest little places she
had ever seen."

Miss Foy was exceedingly pleased with Tiny's
appreciation of her home.

"I am naturally fond of it," she replied, "for I
have watched the growth of every little plant and
shrub in the place, which was really a wilderness
when I first came to it about fifteen years ago.
Philip was then at Eton, and used to come over for
his holidays, so now I tell him he had better come
here for his honeymoon; the Wroughtons will be
away, and the young couple would have the park
all to themselves."

Tiny's face grew very pale ; she gasped out—
"Is Captain Foy going to be married soon ? "
She could not command her voice during a longer
sentence ; it was evident from Miss Foy's last
speech, and previous reference to some unknown
Lady Susan, that some marriage was really in
contemplation.

"Well, I think it will be soon after Christmas ;
and would you believe it, Philip has the face to
complain of waiting so long?   But Lord Fitzwilliam is immovable, and insists upon having his
family about him without any change for another
Christmas-day.   You see," said Miss Foy, who
was always delighted to find any one who would
listen to all she was willing to tell respecting
the nephew she had so helped to spoil, "Master
Phil has such a sad character for the havoc he

makes in the hearts of young ladies, that, I think,
the old earl was thoroughly taken by surprise when
he found Philip had really succumbed to Lady
Susan's charms. You know, my dear," she
added, confidentially, in a lower tone, "soldiers
are very naughty people; they will love and ride
away. I began to think I should never live to see
Philip settle down into a respectable married man."

Tiny made an attempt to say something which
would sound like an appropriate congratulation.
Fortunately for her, Miss Foy was so engrossed
with her own thoughts, that she never noticed the
quivering lips of the pale girl beside her, who fal-
tered out the ordinary phrase expressive of the
ordinary feelings to which people are expected to
give utterance on such occasions. Oh! she
thought, if something would put a stop to this
conversation, and enable her to slip away unobserved to another room; she wanted air, she
wanted—anything to stop this rising in her throat,
which seemed likely to choke her. And still she
yearned to hear all Miss Foy could tell, of the
man who had taken such a hold upon her life.

Thanking Tiny for her kind wishes, Miss Foy
replied that, on the whole, she thought the marriage likely to prove a very satisfactory one, but
she added, " I cannot get over my surprise about
it, for, until I received Philip's letter on Thursday,
announcing the engagement, I had never even
heard him mention Lady Susan in more than a

passing way, and did not know he was going down to stay at Coombe Hall."

At this moment Mr. Philpots took his departure, and the other guests soon followed his example. Mrs. Wroughton then proposed to show the Harewoods their rooms. Miss Foy was already well acquainted with the one assigned to her. It was a small bachelor's room on the ground-floor, which was always placed at her service, to save her the exertion of going up and down stairs.

As Mrs. Wroughton took the girls away, she noticed Tiny's pale face, and its expression of weariness. Laying her hand on her young guest's arm, she rallied her upon her appearance.

"You look as if you wanted another winter of Windsor air, indeed you do. You must allow," she continued, turning to Madeline, "that I sent Tiny home looking all the better for her visit, so I think you ought to trust me with her again. Come, Tiny, what do you say? I am very lonely here in the winter, and it will be quite a charity if you will come and make the house as lively and cheerful as you did before. Oh, how you and Captain Foy used to make us all laugh, and how very badly you did behave to him. I believe he was desperately in love with you, but you snubbed him so unmercifully, you sad little coquette, that you reserved him for an earl's daughter," said Mrs. Wroughton, laughing.

Every vestige of color fled from Tiny's cheeks, and her knees knocked together as she rested a moment against the balustrade.

"Do you know," said Tiny, trying to account, in some reasonable manner, for her sudden indisposition, "I think I am very ill; I ate some Bath buns at the refreshment-room at Slough, and I think they have poisoned me."

Mrs. Wroughton was greatly concerned at Tiny's paleness, but thought the Bath buns were quite sufficient to explain it; one would have been enough to make her uncomfortable, and Tiny talked of them in the plural number, as if they had been so many sugar-plums.

"The little *gourmande* has probably made her luncheon on these horrible indigestible cakes," she said to herself as she hurried to her room, in search of sundry globules which, she assured Tiny, would do her all the good in the world, whether she believed in them or not. Mrs. Wroughton was a devout homœopathist, and was only too eager to seize every opportunity for administering these mysterious little sugar-plums to her friends.

Tiny took the globules upon condition that she should be left alone with her maid, declaring she felt so exceedingly sick, that Mrs. Wroughton and Madeline must go away directly.

When Madeline went back to her sister in half an hour, she found that Pearson had already

9*

tied a pocket-handkerchief steeped in vinegar and water round Tiny's head, closed the shutters, and put out the lights, and but for the faint flickering flame which came from a peculiarly dull fire, the room would have been in total darkness. Madeline groped her way to the sofa, and, as she did so, she heard Tiny sobbing.

" Is your head so bad, Tiny dear ? " she asked, for it was no unusual thing for Tiny to cry if troubled with the slightest physical pain.

" Don't speak to me," she answered ; " it only makes me worse, and I was just going to sleep, and now you have disturbed me ! Do tell Pearson to leave the things," she added impatiently; " she does nothing but tramp up and down the room, till I am nearly frantic. I am sure she had time enough to unpack our trunks while we were talking downstairs."

Madeline understood by the sound of her sister's voice that it would be better to leave her quite alone, so, without answering, she followed the offending Pearson, who was disappearing at that moment with a fresh load of silk dresses into the next room ; and, closing the door behind her, said that Miss Tiny must not be disturbed, and the rest of the things must remain as they were at present.

When Tiny heard the door fairly closed, she gave herself up to the passionate grief she had been forced to repress in the presence of others. It was so strange and cruel, she thought, that here in this very place, so full of the memories of that Winter, where everything reminded her so vividly of her past happiness, and in the dreams in which she had indulged, that she should learn how utterly false and heartless Captain Foy was.

Relieved by the first tears she had dared to shed, Tiny began to reason with herself. After all, it was nothing new, except that at Cowes Captain Foy had again encouraged her belief that he cared a great deal for her, but did not consider his prospects sufficiently good to enable him to marry at present. Otherwise, she had long ago given up all hope, ever since she saw that he did not care to call at Grosvenor Crescent, and rumor had connected his name with Miss Peel.

Before the Roman visit, Tiny had begun to suspect the truth as to Captain Foy's real character. Why, then, did she feel such surprise now? Well, it must be, she supposed, because she had attached too much importance to his attentions on board the yacht, when he appeared once more to yield himself to the pleasure of watching her innocent fair cheeks flush with joy at his approach, and noting the little flutterings by which she betrayed her feeling for him, whenever he managed to steal her hand and hold it in his own for a few minutes.

"Why did he come and stand so close, and look so earnestly into her eyes, if he did not love her?"

And Tiny gave way to another passionate fit of crying.

By this time her poor little head ached in good earnest.

Before Madeline went down to dinner, she helped Pearson to undress her sister, and they left with the understanding that no one should come in until she rang her bell; then Pearson was to bring a cup of tea and some buttered toast.

Tiny very soon sobbed herself to sleep, and did not wake until nearly midnight, long after Madeline had been in her room; Pearson had already been dismissed for the night, after duly providing the teapot, having substituted bread and butter for the toast as less likely to increase her young mistress' bilious headache, so everything was in readiness against the time when Miss Tiny should awake.

As soon as Madeline heard her sister's voice, she carried in the little tray prepared for her. Tiny sat up in bed, and after a strong cup of tea and two pieces of bread and butter, began to feel so much better that she wanted to hear the news; who had been at dinner, what everybody had said, and whether Madeline had talked to Miss Foy?

So Madeline amused Tiny for the next half hour with all the gossip of the evening, including Miss Foy's information about "my nephew and Lady Susan," which she did not in the faintest degree connect with Tiny's violent headache.

Finding her sister knew no more than she did about Captain Foy's intended marriage, Tiny wished her good-night, and resolved to go to sleep without thinking any more of anybody.

Just as a dreamy drowsy sensation was creeping over her, she remembered Wilfred's tenderness and thoughtful love, and prayed that she might be able to give herself up entirely to him, and be made worthy of his generous devotion.

CHAPTER XXVII.

There are loves in man's life for which time can renew
All that time may destroy.

LUCILE.

THE next morning Tiny looked a little paler than usual, but otherwise she seemed in excellent health and spirits. There were several people staying in the house, and what with the walks between the late breakfast and luncheon, and the riding and driving afterwards, with billiards from five-o'clock tea till the dressing bell rang for dinner, whist, and the round games which occupied the evening, there was little or no time for thought. Lady Harewood and Charlotte joined the party at the appointed time, and carried off Madeline and Tiny after a few days' visit, in spite of Mrs. Wroughton's endeavors to persuade the latter to remain a little longer at Windsor.

But Tiny was far too anxious to return to Wilfred. She was longing to talk to him over the altered state of affairs with regard to Captain Foy.

When Wilfred heard of the intended marriage, it appeared to him natural that this intelligence should rekindle all the old interest in Tiny's breast;

and if Captain Foy again engrossed a larger share of their conversation and Tiny's thoughts than Wilfred at all liked, he hoped it was the dying flicker of the lamp before it expired altogether.

And so it proved. Gradually the subject seemed to pain her less ; she talked more reasonably about it than formerly, and at last one day positively amazed Wilfred by laughing over her episode with Captain Foy. She had long ago burnt one or two little notes which he had contrived to send her when he first knew her, and the only memento she retained was a little horseshoe charm, which she now ceased to wear. One day, in a sudden burst of endearment, which reminded Wilfred of those happy days before the Ariel anchored next the Highflyer at Cowes, Tiny threw her arms round his neck, and declared she would not exchange him for fifty Captain Foys.

Wilfred's heart beat tumultuously ; he reaped at last the reward of his long and patient waiting. Taking Tiny in his arms, he held her closely to him, and told her to look up in his face, that he might read in her eyes the same truth her lips had spoken.

When he saw the passionate expression with which Tiny answered him,

> " They kissed so close they could not vow.'

And once more holding her at arm's length and gazing into her face as if to make himself sure of her love, he hastily disengaged himself and left the room.

Now that the sorrow was over, Wilfred Lane realized the heavy strain which had been upon him ever since that evening at Ryde when Tiny confessed the secret she had previously concealed. For a long time he had watched her and tried to sound the depths of her strange character; but whenever he thought he had arrived at an understanding of the different motives which influenced her actions, Tiny would by some curious inconsistency scatter his conclusions to the winds.

One thing only she persistently maintained, namely, that the bond between herself and Wilfred had acquired fresh strength and sanctity from the day on which she confessed to him her attachment for Captain Foy; and she quoted George Eliot in support of her feeling, in these very words: " Every day and night of joy or 'sorrow is a new ground, a new consecration, for the love that is nourished by memories as well as hopes—the love to which perpetual repetition is not a weariness but a want, and to which a separated joy is the beginning of pain."

When Wilfred had seen how Tiny brooded over every incident connected with Captain Foy, how she recalled his looks and tones, how perversely this loving little soul would endow his careless speeches with a meaning and a warmth never acquired from him, he had sometimes feared that she would never cease to care for him. He knew there were souls thus constituted, thus frail and delicate and tender, and he trembled lest his own true passion should fail to recall Tiny to happiness and love.

But in that last embrace she had seemed to assure him that she had lived through her first mistake without having lost the capacity of loving, and after a few weeks of despair the rebound was so great that it carried his hopes at once to the utmost point they had ever reached.

Tiny had really learnt to love him—at last her heart was entirely his own.

Towards the end of January the *Court Circular* devoted two columns and a half to the description of the " marriage in high life of Lady Susan Fitzwilliam and Captain Philip Foy." The ingenious chronicler of that event dwelt *ad nauseam* upon the extreme loveliness of the bride, the gallant devotion of the young and distinguished officer who led her to the hymeneal altar, and the rich and tasteful toilettes of the six noble maidens who officiated as bridemaids. The exquisite and valuable *cadeaux* which the happy and fortunate newly-married pair received as wedding presents from their numerous and aristocratic acquaintances— one and all—were all duly detailed, and the whole affair seemed to afford Tiny a great deal of fun,

until it appeared to Wilfred that she simply regarded it as so much food for merriment.

Certainly he could not accuse her of too much
feeling now ; and but that he was overjoyed at the
change which had lately come over her, he would
have wished that her amusement had been indulged in a quieter and less demonstrative manner. But Tiny had a way of her own about everything, and it was useless to expect that she would
ever act like other people ; and when Wilfred
came to think of it, he never wished to see her
like anything but herself !

The next few weeks were the happiest in Wilfred Lane's life. The black cloud which had
threatened to ingulf him had disappeared ; his
darling seemed to lean entirely on him, and to
find life sweet for his sake. On the first of June
he promised himself that his felicity would be perfect. Day after day, when he reached Grosvenor
Crescent, he saw Tiny's little face pressed against
the library window, in order that she might catch
the first glimpse of her lover as soon as he came in
sight ; and both began to count the days which
divided them from that on which Lady Harewood
had promised her consent to their marriage.
Tiny repeatedly assured Wilfred that her life was
bound up in him, and Wilfred certainly had no
thought apart from Tiny, and could imagine no
future of which she was not the central figure.

CHAPTER XXVIII.

"Hopes, what are they?   Beads of morning
Strung on slender blades of grass ;
Or a spider's web adorning   ·
In a strait and treacherous pass."

WORDSWORTH.

IN the middle of March, Tiny went with Lady
Harewood on a few days' visit to General and
Lady Isabella Drummond.   Her mother insisted
on taking Tiny to Bellingham Castle, because she
heard that Sir Guy Fairfax would be there ; and
she felt the time was drawing near when her favorite scheme must be relinquished altogether, unless
Sir Guy was aided, both speedily and effectually,
in his pursuit of Tiny's hand.

Tiny left London in happy ignorance of her
mother's intentions, which were, however, destined to meet with signal disappointment ; for, on
reaching the Castle, Lady Harewood discovered
Sir Guy was not expected until the very day on
which she and Tiny were to take their departure.
Her mortification was extreme ; and so was her
rage against Lady Isabella, whom she secretly accused of machinations to entrap the wealthy young

baronet " for one of those tall, gawky girls of hers, about whom she made such a ridiculous fuss."

Tiny and the Miss Drummonds had always been on the best of terms; indeed, it was very difficult for any one to resist Tiny's coaxing ways, which perfectly bewitched men, and so fascinated the ladies of her acquaintance, that she generally escaped being judged by the ordinary standard. This was certainly very fortunate for Miss Tiny Harewood, for she was in the habit of saying and doing in one day more daring and unconventional things than most young ladies would venture upon in the whole course of their lives.

The Drummonds were getting up some private theatricals which were to take place the week after Easter, and to be followed by a dance. Tiny was soon pressed into the service; and, after much reflection on the part of Lady Harewood as to the probable result of leaving her, it was arranged that she should stay on at Bellingham Castle after her mother's departure, in order to take her part in the necessary rehearsals. Lady Harewood and her other daughters were to come for the second performance of the play, which was to be given on two consecutive nights. The Drummonds' visiting list was so extensive, that no amount of crushing would have enabled them on one night to receive all the people they " ought to ask," and the old General was very particular in never allowing the miniature theatre to be overcrowded.

The play selected was "The Hunchback;" and
Modus was the part assigned to Reginald Macnaghten, Lady Isabella's nephew, a young lieutenant in
the Guards.   Until Tiny's arrival the Miss Drummonds could not agree as to who would best acquit
herself as *Helen;* but, with one accord, they fixed
upon her, declaring that she would act the part to
perfection.   Tiny at first scrupled to undertake the
representation of this forward young damsel, and
hesitated about making the necessary overtures to
Mr. Macnaghten in his character of *Modus;* but
the girls assured her that, as their cousin was as
good as engaged to a certain Miss Lucy Scott,
there could be no possible objection to her making
love to him in the play.   So all lingering doubts
or objections on Wilfred's account were dismissed.
Tiny learnt her part; the different scenes were re-
hearsed; and the days were spent in preparation
for the grand performance which was to crown
their labors.

At first, Mr. Reginald Macnaghten was not over
pleased with the idea of Tiny Harewood as *Helen.*
He made this as apparent as he could, with any
show of politeness, before the young lady herself,
and expressed his disapproval openly to Gertrude
and Isabel Drummond: but they fired up so vehemently in defence of Tiny's capability of doing
full justice to the part assigned her, that young
Macnaghten perceived that it was a settled thing,
and he must make the best of it.

At the very first rehearsal, however, he was
forced to acknowledge the wisdom of his cousins'
choice ; and, before long, the curious dominion
Tiny exerted over men, which made them go down
on their knees at once, became apparent in the
young Guardsman's case.　His manner in the final
love-making scene became a great deal too earnest
and life-like, and the whole position enabled him
to assume an intimacy with Tiny Harewood which
was (to say the least of it) extremely dangerous
for both.

Is it not Thackeray who remarks that it is " fortunate for men that women, like the beasts of the
field, don't know their own power; they would
overcome men entirely if they did " ?　Perhaps it
was Tiny's accurate measurement of her own attractions which made them so peculiarly fatal !

A great deal went on before any one noticed the
flirtation ; and when the girls first saw how completely *épris* their cousin was, they considered it
excellent fun, and a righteous judgment upon that
young gentleman for the slighting manner in which
he had at first spoken of Tiny.　Lady Isabella was
the last to remark the state of affairs, but when she
did observe it she was not inclined to interfere with
either of her guests.　Tiny's position with regard
to Wilfred Lane was unknown to her ; and she
thought it always much wiser, in such matters, to
let things take their own course.　Besides, Tiny
carried on her part of the flirtation in such an ex-

ceedingly open fashion, that Lady Isabella doubted
if she had any real feeling for Reginald Macnaghten ; and as for him, he was old enough to manage
his own affairs.   If his attachment for Lucy Scott
was of so slight a nature, why, it was better for
the poor girl to find it out before marriage than
after.

So Miss Tiny Harewood and the young Guardsman had it all their own way.

Tiny quickly perceived that Mr. Macnaghten
had not in the first instance evinced a due appreciation of her charms, so she resolved to bring him
into proper subjection ; and it must be confessed
she effected this with a rapidity which even astonished herself.   When Tiny determined to fascinate
a man she seldom failed to accomplish it ; and was
scarcely likely to do so in the case of one so inex-
perienced as her present admirer, whose feeling for
Lucy Scott was but the first sentimental affection
of a mere boy.

Tiny was not so heartless as to have any definite
intention of bringing pain to the girl, who all this
while cherished a belief in an affection which was
sensibly diminishing before the bright glances of
another.   But she was utterly thoughtless.

> "And evil is wrought by want of thought
> As well as by want of heart."

Reginald Macnaghten's indifference during the
first days of their acquaintance, had fired her with

the old love of conquest; and her vanity and love
of admiration were insatiable.   Now that she allowed the old spirit to assert itself, it did so with
renewed vigor, and after a few days Tiny seemed
to lose all power of controlling it, and was soon in
the midst of a flirtation which threatened to exceed
even those in which she had indulged the season
before she accepted the love of her cousin, and
promised to regard herself as his affianced wife.

Wilfred Lane was not there to influence her ; and
as no one at Bellingham Castle interfered, these
young people afforded a great deal of amusement
to the whole circle of their friends, and were quite
undisturbed in the plans they daily made for their
mutual entertainment.   If Tiny rode, it was looked
upon as a settled thing that Reginald would also
ride ; and it followed as a natural consequence,
that, when the riding party divided into pairs,
Reginald and Tiny fell behind and kept at a distance, which was by no means as necessary for the
convenience of the rest of the party as their own.
If Tiny walked, Reginald's horse was counter-
manded ; and if he did not actually take her in to
dinner, somehow or other they always found
themselves side by side.

Sir Guy Fairfax came down at the appointed
time, and left in despair.   He could never get a
word with Tiny " for that confounded puppy Macnaghten ; " and began to weary of this fruitless
pursuit of a girl who seemed utterly indifferent to

attractions readily enough appreciated by most of the young ladies of his acquaintance.

General Drummond and Wilfred's father had been great friends in early life; and, as it was no uncommon event for Wilfred to spend a few days at Bellingham Castle, it excited no surprise, when Lady Isabella announced at breakfast one morning, that she had invited him to join the party on the following Saturday.

Tiny was absolutely delighted when she heard Wilfred was coming; and not only gave full vent to her feelings in public, but privately indited a note, begging him to remain over the Monday if he could get leave of absence, because Monday was the day for the first dress rehearsal, and she wanted him to be present above everything.

In the meantime Mr. Macnaghten's feeling for Tiny was fast passing all bounds; and, whenever they were alone, she had enough to do to laugh away his serious speeches. It taxed her ingenuity not a little, to keep him to the absurd and ridiculous style they assumed towards each other in public. Once or twice Reginald had been on the point of declaring his affection for her, but as, in her opinion, this would have spoilt the whole affair, Tiny kept such a firm hand over him, that he feared to risk his position by a premature avowal, conscious that, at present, Tiny would cut the matter short, and thus bring to an end their free and pleasant intercourse.

10

So he contented himself by giving Tiny to understand, as far as he dared, that he was resolved to wait, in the hope of inducing her some day to return the affection she had inspired *malgré lui* in his own breast. He even alluded to Lucy Scott, when he found that Tiny was in possession of his little secret, and assured her that no engagement had ever existed between them, and that he should "pitch into his cousins for such an unwarrantable use of Miss Scott's name, at the first possible opportunity." Mr. Reginald Macnaghten was discovering that "absence makes the heart grow fonder—*of somebody else.*"

It was all very well to assure Tiny Harewood that he had never loved Lucy Scott; but the young lieutenant was somewhat troubled in his own mind about his conduct. He felt himself in an awkward position; for Miss Scott and he had exchanged sundry words which he now wished altogether expunged from her memory. He was not engaged to her; but he knew he had taken as much trouble last summer to secure the confiding heart of that quiet retiring girl, as he was now bestowing to capture this provoking little butterfly, who seemed to elude him just when he made most sure of winning her; and who yet continued to draw him on in a manner which so tantalized him, that more than once he was on the point of losing his well-sustained control, and risking his fate by an immediate declaration.

Tiny's interest in the arrival of Mr. Wilfred Lane was by no means pleasing to her present adorer, who never felt less inclined to obey her commands than he did on that Saturday afternoon, when she requested him to gather a fresh sprig of ivy from the wall they were passing, because her cousin liked her to wear it in her hair in preference to all the wreaths which ever came out of Regent Street.

His displeasure amounted to absolute exasperation when the gentleman in question made his appearance. True to his promise to Lady Harewood, Mr. Lane was guarded in society, in order to prevent his real position with his cousin being remarked upon. But the eyes of a jealous lover were too keen to be deceived by a disguise which did well enough for the rest of the world ; and, in spite of all caution, there was a quiet sense of ownership in Wilfred's manner with Tiny, which perfectly infuriated Macnaghten. He thought, too, that Tiny seemed afraid of Lane ; doubtless he exercised some authority over her, for Reginald noticed that she avoided him after Lane's arrival, and for the first time purposely went to the other side of the table at dinner, and transferred all her attentions to this odious cousin.

Mr. Macnaghten considered himself aggrieved, and not unnaturally hated Wilfred Lane from the bottom of his soul. After the ladies retired, he sat opposite his enemy, cracking nuts, and feeling there was no injury in the world he would not do him if a benevolent providence ever placed it in his power.   Quite unconsciously Wilfred increased the young man's wrath ; noticing Macnaghten's silence, and attributing it to shyness, he tried to draw him into conversation, which Reginald mistook for malicious condescension, and resented accordingly.

During the evening Tiny was asked to sing ; Wilfred, being near the piano-forte, opened it for his cousin, and helped her to find her music (which was of course in confusion and in everybody's portfolio   instead   of   her   own).   Macnaghten watched them ; scowling at Wilfred with a rising anger, which nearly burst all bounds when the latter in his quiet easy manner removed the song before Tiny, and insisted on her singing one selected by himself from the mass of music before them.

" The cool impudent beggar ! " muttered the disconcerted Macnaghten between his teeth ; " how she can stand his interference I can't think. If I asked for a particular song, it would be quite enough to make her say it was the very one which did not suit her voice."

When Tiny finished singing " *Dove sono,*" Reginald found every fault he could think of with it, in a way which Wilfred thought exceedingly rude. Tiny was secretly amused ; she knew well enough what was passing in both their minds, and resolved to excite the indignation of her youthful admirer still more ; so she paid no attention to his remarks, but, turning to Wilfred, asked him to sing her favorite song by Hatton, "To Anthea who may command him anything," the accompaniment of which she knew ·by heart ; Wilfred did not understand much about music. He was a little too fond of taking his "own time" to please Tiny ; but then he had a pleasant voice and a perfect ear, and his enunciation was so clear and distinct that his singing was generally liked. On the present occasion he did full justice to this spirited song ; and when Macnaghten saw the glance he gave Tiny as he came to the words—

> "Thou art my life, my soul, my heart,
> The very eyes of me ;
> And hast command of every part
> To live and die for thee "—

which he sang with intense feeling, Reginald thought he should like "to pitch the confounded fellow out of the window, and the music-stool after him."

As the proprieties of the nineteenth century forbade this summary way of proceeding, he was forced to content himself with the observation that he thought "the accompaniment extremely loud and noisy ; and the words the most foolish he had ever heard in his life," leaving Mr. Lane wavering between doubts as to the sanity of this young man, and a growing conviction that Mr. Reginald Mac-

naghten was, without exception, the rudest and
most ill-mannered individual in Her Majesty's service !

When the music ceased, whist was proposed,
and Wilfred was placed at a table with General
Drummond, Mrs. Wilmot (a pretty young widow
staying in the house), and Miss Robertson, who
was dining there with her father that evening ; not
far off was another quartett, composed of Gertrude,
Tiny, Captain Reynolds, and Reginald.

Now that Wilfred was at some little distance,
and Tiny resumed her old playful manner, Reginald began to thaw ; indeed it would have been a
difficult task for a more ill-tempered man than he
was to remain sulky under the influence of the fun
and merriment Tiny Harewood always introduced
at cards—much to the displeasure of graver people,
who generally seem to regard whist as a serious
game, in which their reputations as well as their
purses are at stake, objecting to the utterance of a
single unnecessary word during the whole game.
Tiny openly avowed that she abhorred such so-
lemnity,—she hated whist unless allowed to cheat
and talk as much as she pleased ! With or without permission Tiny's tongue seldom stopped ;
and she certainly neglected no opportunity of looking over her neighbor's cards, and proclaiming,
for the benefit of the entire party, the trump card
she discovered in an opponent's hand.

It was now Wilfred's turn to look somewhat

eagerly across the room to the table from which
all this fun and merriment proceeded; and it required no small effort on his part to conceal how
fearfully his own game bored him. During the
last rubber he made a mis-deal; twice he failed to
return his partner's lead; and once, to Mrs. Wilmot's great disgust, he nearly trumped her trick.
To his relief the third rubber at last came to an
end; and, paying up his losses, Wilfred rose, in
order, as he said, to make room for a better
player. So Mr. Robertson, encouraged by Mr.
Lane's misfortune (yet declaring himself no player
at all), ventured to hope Mrs. Wilmot would accept him as Wilfred's substitute, and that he should
help her to retrieve her past ill-luck.

Wilfred Lane strolled to the other table, and
stood behind Macnaghten, watching the game.
His familiarity with Tiny was extremely distasteful
to Wilfred; and the way in which he addressed her
as "partner" did not at all diminish the dislike
which the young man's rudeness had already excited.

When the ladies left the drawing-rooms, Gertrude took such firm possession of his cousin that
Wilfred saw he had no chance of a word with her
unobserved by the company at large; so he said
good-night to them both, his eyes resting with a
loving longing expression upon Tiny. Just as
they reached the door, Reginald Macnaghten
jumped up, and catching hold of Gertrude's arm,

to Wilfred's great annoyance left the room with the two girls.

Some minutes later, when Wilfred crossed the hall with General Drummond on the way to the billiard room, he looked up and saw Tiny and Gertrude still talking on the staircase to this obnoxious little Guardsman ; and heard him say, as he turned from Tiny—with a gesture and familiarity which absolutely enraged him—

> " Her lips *shall* be in danger
> When next she trusts them near me ! "

Wilfred Lane knew all about the play ; but, in his anger, it did not occur to him that Mr. Macnaghten's speech was a simple quotation.

It was, perhaps, well for all parties that only Captain Reynolds joined the billiard players that night, and that Mr. Lane's anger had time to expend itself on the unlimited number of cigars which he smoked before he went to bed.

CHAPTER XXIX.

"Sundaies the pillars are
   On which heav'n's palace arched lies;
   The other dayes fill up the spare
   And hollow room with vanities.

   .   .   .   .   .

The Sundaies of man's life,
   Thredded together on time's string,
   Make bracelets to adorn the wife
   Of the eternall glorious King.
   On Sunday heaven's gate stands ope;
   Blessings are plentifull and rife,
   More plentifull than hope."
                                    GEORGE HERBERT.

BREAKFAST at Bellingham Castle on Sunday morning was always at nine, instead of ten o'clock. Lady Isabella Drummond wished her servants to go to church, and this could scarcely be managed unless the rooms were vacated at an earlier hour than usual. So the gong sounded as the clock in the turret struck nine. As it did so, Wilfred Lane opened the door of the gallery which led on to the general staircase from the set of rooms in which his own was situated; and Tiny did precisely the same at the opposite end. Seeing Wil-

10*

fred she ran towards him, exclaiming in her bright
and joyous way—

"The top of the morning to you, Wil, dear.
Isn't this a pleasant house ?   I am so happy here ;
now you have come, it's perfect."

"I think you made yourself very comfortable
before," replied Wilfred, with a shadow of cold-
ness in his tone, for he could not forget last night's
episode ; it had rankled in his mind ever since.

"Now, Mr. Gravity," said Tiny—linking herself on his arm with both hands, and looking up
into his face, with an expression which set his heart
off thumping as quickly as ever—"you don't wish
your little wife to be as sober as a judge before
she really takes upon herself the fearful responsibility of keeping you in order?   Come, Wil," she
added in a pleading voice, which touched his heart
directly, "I have not been so very light-hearted
lately, that you need reproach me because my
spirits run away with me now I find myself with
girls of my own age."

The gallery door opened again as Tiny spoke,
and Gertrude and Isabel appeared ; as they
greeted one another, Wilfred Lane was calling
himself hard names, for his want of generosity in
having harbored such ill-conditioned thoughts
about Tiny ; and, in his genial pleasant manner,
he began to make amends for it, by talking to the
three girls as they went down the stairs together
into the pleasant breakfast room ; which looked

.cheerful enough, until young Macnaghten thrust himself into the very seat next Tiny which Wilfred was standing by, and intended to occupy.

The facetious conversation which ensued annoyed Wilfred exceedingly. He had seldom seen Tiny in this kind of mood; and it was so infinitely. below the rest of her character, that it grated upon his taste and sense of propriety. Young Macnaghten's noisy mirth, and the nonsense they talked, seemed but little in accordance with the quiet Sunday morning, which was always a double rest, in the country, to this man who worked half the night, as well as all the day, in London. Wilfred Lane made it a rule, from which he seldom deviated, to keep one day out of the seven clear from the working atmosphere of the rest; and as free from care and anxiety as he could make it. Breathless ·and weary with the labors of the past week, and the full weight of the world's temptations, he had looked forward to this special day, as one from which he should gain fresh strength and hope; and anything more discordant than this foolish flippant jesting could scarcely be conceived. He walked round the table, and took the vacant seat between Gertrude Drummond and Mrs. Wilmot; very nearly opposite to Tiny and her companion.

Several times he found himself looking at them with positive amazement; for their absurdity was unredeemed by any particular wit or originality,

and it appeared to Wilfred only fit for the nursery
or school-room.

It was no relief to see that the Drummonds were
accustomed to this style of behavior: nor was he
better pleased when Mrs. Wilmot remarked with
a significant nod, "What a charming cousin you
have, Mr. Lane, and what a perfect little coquette !
She has quite turned poor Reginald Macnaghten's
head ; and I don't think she really means to be
merciful to him in the end."

Wilfred stammered out some answer about Tiny's
amazing life and spirits, and her extraordinary
powers of attraction ; but he differed from Mrs.
Wilmot in calling her a coquette, " for any one
less conscious of her powers of fascination he never
saw ; " a remark which considerably diminished
Mrs. Wilmot's respect for his judgment, and somewhat jarred against a conviction which was gaining
strength in his own mind.

As the church was at some little distance, the
open carriage started from the hall-door at half-
past ten ; and those who liked to walk followed
rather later, as they could take a short cut through
the shrubbery, and across the deer park.

Tiny was a great walker ; and, a few minutes
after the less active members of the party had
driven off, she appeared with Gertrude and Mrs.
Wilmot. They were at once joined by the gentlemen who had made up their minds to go to
church—a resolution which was confined to Wil-

fred, Captain Reynolds, and young Macnaghten, whose attraction was neither the service nor the sermon, but the prospect of a walk with Miss Tiny Harewood.

The ladies went in single file through the shrubberies, and, in crossing the park, they were all together, so the conversation was pretty evenly distributed ; and the fresh, pleasant country air gave Wilfred such a sense of enjoyment, that, by the time they reached the quaint little country church, all traces of annoyance had disappeared ; his eyes were resting lovingly upon his cousin, and he was longing for the time when her acknowledged position would prevent any man from taking the shadow of a liberty with one who had promised to love and honor him alone.

The pew belonging to the Castle was reached by outer steps, which led into a comfortable square room, with a huge fireplace at one end, and luxurious arm-chairs all round. It was no wonder that when the General did come to church, he always went fast asleep during the second lesson, and seldom awoke till the sermon was ended ; even Lady Isabella declared that the walls of Bellingham Church were sown with poppy seed, and the curate's voice was " somnolent and sleep-compelling."

Wilfred hated these kind of pews ; they seemed to him to spoil the meaning of the beautiful Church Service, which calls together " rich and poor, one with another," into the presence of their Maker, as brethren in this world, and heirs together of one blessed home in the world to come.

He had not the least tendency to ritualism, for he could not endure the introduction of practices which appeared to him to make the heart sad of those whom God had not made sad, and laid burdens upon men, grievous to be borne, and increased in an unnatural manner the distance between the soul of man and its Maker.

Perhaps he could scarcely be called a good churchman ; though he belonged to the Church of England, and nothing would have induced him to quit her communion, for he loved her noble Book of Prayer, which is so catholic and so comprehensive, and so much in advance of the practice of the Church.

He liked, too, the open churches and their free seats, where all mingled together without respect of persons ; he cared, too, that the music should be of the best and highest description—such as might really elevate the hearts of those who wished to sing to the honor and glory of God— and it always grated against his sense of the fitness of things, when he heard (as you yet may in too many English country churches) the hymn given out by an illiterate clerk (whose mispronunciation would spoil the best words which were ever written), and sung by a congregation who neither care

nor know whether they keep to the tune they attempt to sing or not.

The service on the morning in question was
very well performed ; the chants and anthem were
sung with real feeling and without display ; the
prayers were read by a curate, who was devout
without being unctuous ; and the hymn—

> "Nearer, my God, to Thee,
> Nearer to Thee,
> E'en though it be a cross
> That raiseth me—"

which preceded the sermon, was a special favorite, and one which often came back to Wilfred in
after days, when he remembered the quiet service
in this little country church.

The sermon was preached by a stranger, and
addressed particularly to the younger members of
the congregation, who were preparing for confir-
mation. The preacher warned them that they
had in a special sense their choice to make, and
that the complexion of their after life depended
very much upon the line of conduct they adopted
during this period—not because their younger
days were likely to be more sinful than those of
after life, for each time had its special sins, and
perhaps the less prominent sins of later years are
even more hateful in the sight of God.

He implored the young men who were present,
to believe that the enemies of their souls were real

and very deadly; that "the world is an enemy, with its temptation to set the affections on things beneath, not on things above; to have the mind choked up by worldly ambitions—the eyes dazzled with the sight of the kingdoms of this world and the glory of them—a temptation of which every middle-aged man in that church would confess the power, and of which perhaps nearly each had experienced the danger."

"The flesh," he continued, with increased earnestness, "is a real enemy, and an enemy in the camp; one, moreover, which will assail us under the most insinuating disguises, and which finds special strength and support in the ardent temperament of young blood. The devil, too, is a real enemy—never believe that the devil is a fiction, but regard him as the most awful of facts. Here, then, I say, are real enemies, and who shall overestimate their power? Young men and women! These are terrible enemies if any there be; and that was God's truth in which you were baptized, where you were pledged with the sign of Christ's cross to fight against them. And what I desire to impress upon you is, that you can only fight successfully by ruling yourselves according to the Word of God. Let me beg of you to mark those words, *ruling yourselves*—implying, as I conceive, that constant drill which makes the soldier—constant discipline—constant energy in doing good—not implying a few good

resolutions now and then—not implying mere
religious fits; fits of exercise never yet made a
soldier, and fits of religious feelings will never
make a soldier of Christ."

When they came out of church, Wilfred Lane
felt but little disposed to talk. Several words in
the sermon had come home to him with such
power, that he was unable to shake off the
thoughts they brought as soon as he crossed the
church portal.

But he was obliged, like Felix, to put them
aside for " a more convenient season," and to help
the ladies with their sundry wraps and books into
the carriage, which was waiting at the farther end
of the churchyard—then he joined the walkers.

Though he took no share in the conversation on
the way home, it disturbed and distracted him.

" Now, that is a nice kind of sermon," said the
sprightly little widow; " I can't bear all those
long discourses about ' predestination ' and ' bap-
tismal regeneration.' "

" No," said Captain Reynolds; " those are
things, as Lord Dundreary would say, ' no feller
can be expected to understand.' "

" Well—I liked it, because it was short," said
Gertrude; " Mr. Williamson sometimes preaches
for an hour, and by the time I come out of church
I have forgotten even the text he began with."

" You would like to have ' sat under ' Peter
Pindar, perhaps; " exclaimed Reginald Mac-

naghten—eagerly seizing the opportunity of bringing in a favorite story of his, which he never lost the chance of telling, since he heard it two years before. "Did you ever hear, Miss Harewood, of a sermon preached by that celebrated divine on the text 'Man is born to trouble as the sparks fly upwards'?"

Tiny said she had not; so he continued—"Well, if you don't know it, and it isn't long, I must repeat it to you. 'Dearly beloved brethren; I am going to preach to-day from the verse "Man is born to trouble as the sparks fly upwards," and I shall divide my sermon into three heads:

"'I.   Man's ingress into the world.

"'II.   Man's progress through the world.

"'III.   Man's egress out of the world.

"'I. Man's ingress into the world—naked and bare. II. Man's progress through the world—trouble and care. III. Man's egress out of the world—no one knows where; and if I were to preach for a year I could tell you nothing more—so now—Amen.'"

Of course, every one laughed when Mr. Macnaghten concluded, and Peter Pindar's point and brevity were duly appreciated. But, when Mrs. Wilmot proceeded to remark upon the profanity attributed to that departed worthy, Tiny, watching her opportunity, slipped away from the others to join Wilfred, who was walking a little apart from the rest.

Gradually they fell behind, and began to talk of what was uppermost in both their minds.

Tiny, too, had listened to the sermon, and it had made its impression on her; for the moment she felt forced to acknowledge that the power of ruling herself was precisely what she most needed. She had a wonderful way of analyzing her own character, and of seeing its defects, but there she stopped. Sometimes, indeed, she made a few valiant resolutions, but the first temptation put them all to flight. Changeable in temperament, she often seemed worse and often better than she really was; but her unsteadiness in the small matters of life, and her want of ballast, undermined her good intentions before she was aware of it. When Tiny Harewood was a few years younger, Wilfred used to say of her that she was like " Milton's Eve, the type of the masculine standard of perfection in women; a graceful figure, an abundance of fine hair, much coy submission, and such a degree of unreasoning wilfulness as shall risk perdition."

There was only one point to which Tiny remained constant—her affection for Wilfred. This, she protested, was based upon the deeper part of her mind; his love was essential to her.

At the time of their first separation she had been so long under Wilfred's immediate influence, that she continued to live in the atmosphere of the high and noble thoughts and interests he was

gradually developing in her. But, on her return
to London, the difficulty of her position with Wilfred, and the want of an elevated tone in her
mother's house, added to her own love of perpetual "change," kept fallow a soil which Nature
had endowed with her richest gifts.   Tiny's good
aspirations were at first allowed to rove at large,
and finally devoted to vanity and frivolity, until
her whole being succumbed to the first temptation
which assailed her.   In the present instance this
met her in the form of a flirtation with a lively
young man, over whom she consciously exerted
her power in a way which she knew to be unworthy of her better self, and inconsistent with
her position with Wilfred Lane.

The sermon to-day had aroused her to a fresh
sense of this; and when she came up to her
cousin and took his arm, she did so with a firm
resolution to alter her manner towards Reginald
Macnaghten from that very moment.   But she did
not feel disposed to own as much as this to Wilfred, not even when he expressed his annoyance
at the foolish bantering tone she allowed Macnaghten to assume, which was so ill in keeping
with the tie existing between them.   Tiny felt the
justice of his reproof; but her wilful little spirit
rebelled against his plain unvarnished condemnation of her conduct; and she resented his express-
ing the very thoughts which were passing through
her own mind.

Wilfred Lane's patience and tenderness over Tiny's waywardness about Captain Foy had been unbounded; but this was a very different sort of thing, and he gave Tiny to understand he would by no means tolerate it.

CHAPTER XXX.

" Right thro' his manful breast darted the pang
That makes a man, in the sweet face of her
Whom he loves most, lonely and miserable."
Idylls of the King.

TINY HARE WOOD was extremely quiet throughout the whole of luncheon. She was either con-
vinced by what Wilfred had said, or else, having
found the censure already administered exceedingly unpalatable, she feared to provoke another.
Her conscience told her how little Wilfred knew
all that had taken place, and how thoroughly
she deserved his condemnation.

Of course this alteration in Tiny's behavior was
not lost on Mr. Macnaghten. Nor was he back-
ward in attributing it to the interference of that
" conceited prig of a cousin, who was so dull and
morose himself that he hated to see other people
jolly enough to enjoy themselves." And the
young Lieutenant registered a vow that if ever
Miss Tiny Harewood became " Mrs. Reginald
Macnaghten," as he fondly believed she ultimately
would, that " kill-joy-fellow " should never darken
his doors, if he could help it. He glanced

fiercely at Mr. Lane, longing to deliver Tiny out of his clutches.

It must be confessed that Wilfred did not appear at this moment to advantage at Bellingham Castle. Naturally of an easy and genial temperament, his friends were surprised at a taciturn and crude manner most unusual to him. His disapproval of the intimacy between Tiny and Mr. Macnaghten was evident to the Drummonds; but, being ignorant of the real tie between the cousins, they were unable to understand his conduct, and felt inclined to resent it as most unreasonable.

Never had an exhortation to "rule himself" come at a more seasonable time to Wilfred; for he felt very angry with Tiny, exceedingly sore with Reginald Macnaghten, and hurt at the suspicions entertained by his friends.

When Tiny made him miserable on board the yacht, there was a depth and earnestness about the matter which drew out the finer parts of her character and claimed a certain kind of respect. In the present instance, however, Wilfred had a very different sort of feeling, in which respect did not mingle in the least.

There was something so peculiarly aggressive in Macnaghten's manner towards himself personally, that Wilfred almost lost sight of the fact that the young man was unconsciously injuring him by his attentions to his affianced wife; and perhaps Wilfred did not care to open his eyes to what made Tiny's share in the blame so much the heavier.

Lady Isabella Drummond next came in for a share of his displeasure. He thought her wrong to countenance her nephew's open admiration of a young guest left completely under her protection. The least she could have done would have been to compel Reginald to cease from making a conspicuous display of his feeling for Tiny: and, as these thoughts passed through his mind, he became moody and silent.

When he had finished blaming the whole party, he began to condemn himself; for he was fond of the Drummonds, and hated himself for having hard thoughts of the people by whom he was surrounded, and of whose hospitality he was partaking.

Finding Tiny surrounded by the girls in the drawing-room after luncheon, he resolved to go for a long walk. He was indisposed for any company but his own, and hoped that exercise might disperse the ill-conditioned state of mind in which he found himself. So off he started, unobserved by any one; thinking of Tiny the whole time, he paid no heed to the direction he took, and walked so far that the first bell had already rung when he returned, and there was scarcely time to dress for dinner.

Tiny, too, had been revolving matters in her own mind, during the short time she had been alone. But first of all she had accompanied the old General and his daughters to the stables, where the horses were duly inspected, according to the regular Sunday-afternoon practice, and a piece of sugar administered to each with scrupulous impartiality. Then they made the tour of the kitchen gardens and forcing houses ; after which Tiny Harewood retired with Gertrude and heard certain confidences touching Horace Alvanley, who had been for some time paying her very marked attention.

It was wonderful, considering the frank and open manner Tiny possessed, to see how very closely she could keep her own concerns to herself, while she gave people the impression of always saying whatever was passing in her mind. Tiny never allowed a human being to know her one bit more intimately than she thought convenient; and on this occasion she considered it was better for her friends to know nothing of her engagement to Wilfred Lane. She even allowed Gertrude to remark how much more self-engrossed Wilfred appeared, and how far less agreeable he was than usual, and still refrained from giving her friend the key to her cousin's conduct.

At the same time, next to feeling out of conceit with herself, she was really vexed at the unfavora-.ble impression Wilfred was making upon everybody ; but she was selfish enough to be still more sore with his plain condemnation of her own con-

11

duct, and not at all disposed to overlook his absenting himself the whole afternoon ; this she regarded as a great slight to herself, and exceedingly rude to everybody.

Tiny went down to dinner with a wicked little demon sitting in the coils of her beautiful hair, prompting her to all kinds of extravagance, with plausible reasons attached to each. If she altered her manner to Reginald while Wilfred was in the house, it suggested she would make matters infinitely worse ; not only would every one accuse her of fearing her cousin, but they would attribute to her conduct a greater degree of blame than she considered it deserved ; or else Wilfred would be placed in the odious position of a marplot. Next the little demon whispered that, by making herself doubly agreeable, she would not only atone for Wilfred's behavior, but divert attention from him by directing it to herself.

While the servants were in the room things went on pretty quietly ; but at dessert Tiny astonished them all, and yet was so exceedingly original and daring that it was impossible for any one but Wilfred to refrain from laughing.

After dinner, the gentlemen adjourned to the smoking room ; for, a long Sunday evening, without whist or music, induced them to postpone their entrance into the drawing-room to an unusually late hour.

Lady Isabella objected to music on a Sunday,

because her mother had done so before her ; and
the girls had tried in vain to introduce sacred
music by Handel and Mozart, which would not
only have relieved the tedium of those evenings,
but might have supplied the very spiritual element
of which they were so sadly destitute.

When Wilfred entered the drawing-room, about
half-past nine o'clock, he found Tiny and Mr.
Macnaghten seated on a sofa, with a large photo-
graph book into which they were looking ; or
rather, behind which they were talking.

Tiny looked uncomfortable when she saw the
expression of her cousin's face ; and this was immediately attributed by Reginald to her imagined
fear of Lane, who appeared to him to act the
mentor over her in a most unwarrantable manner.

"You seem very much afraid of Mr. Secretary
Lane," said Reginald, while pretending to look
at another page ; " for my part I hate fellows who
think such a lot of themselves, and interfere with
other people's affairs."

"Indeed, I'm not in the least afraid of him.
Wilfred is the best creature in the world," she
added ; coming, with a true woman's instinct, to the
defence of the man she loved directly any one
attacked him.

This did not mitigate Macnaghten's wrath, and
he ventured on another depreciatory remark, which
Tiny effectually silenced by rising from her seat
and saying she did not care to look at any more

photographs.   She went to Wilfred, and in a low
voice asked him not to look so cross.

Wilfred was conscious of feeling exceedingly
savage.   He was indignant with Tiny for raising
up, in his own nature, passions he heartily de-
spised—and he was rendered still more angry,
when, in answer to the reply he made her, Tiny
told him that the whole thing arose from his being
" so ridiculously jealous and disagreeable to the
poor boy, that she was forced to be extra kind
and amiable to make up for his want of manners."

A stronger expression and nearer to an oath
than Wilfred Lane was at all in the habit of using,
escaped from his lips, as Tiny uttered this mean
and ungenerous subterfuge.

Bound by the peculiar circumstances of his
promise to Lady Harewood, he was forced to accept one of the most intolerable positions in which
any one can be placed.

No honorable man could stand quietly by, and
see the girl to whom he is pledged suffer another
to approach her with attentions which would not
be offered her as his wife.   The very concealment
of the tie between them only made it more wrong
of Tiny to take advantage of such a position.   It
was for her to check Macnaghten's advances, not
to encourage them as if she were free to receive all
he might feel disposed to offer.

The long-suffering that Wilfred had shown in
the matter of Captain Foy, only made him less

inclined to take a lenient view of Tiny's present conduct. She ought to have learnt from her own sorrow something of the pain she had inflicted upon him ; and when her feeling for Captain Foy ceased, and she refused to accept the freedom Wilfred had pressed upon her, he felt he had a right to expect that this girl—for whose love he had waited so patiently and for whom he had suffered ,so much—should cleave to him with her whole heart and soul. To find her amusing herself by a flirtation with Reginald Macnaghten thoroughly roused his indignation ; and, for the first time in his life, Wilfred Lane was not only angry with Tiny, but a shadow of disgust crept into the feeling with which he had hitherto regarded her. As he stood, apparently turning over the leaves of a book which lay on the table beside him, his whole soul was in a tumult—

> " For, to be wroth with one we love,
> Doth work like madness on the brain."

CHAPTER XXXI.

"People who love downy peaches are not apt to think of the stone, and sometimes jar their teeth terribly against it.
GEORGE ELIOT.

WHEN Tiny came down to breakfast the next morning she found to her amazement that Wilfred had already left for London.

Late on the previous night, while smoking with General Drummond, he suddenly remembered some important papers which required to be despatched without delay. Never suspecting Wilfred's real motive, the General proposed to send a telegram ; but on Wilfred's assurance that no one could find the despatches but himself, it was arranged that the dog-cart should be ready at eight o'clock, in time to catch the morning express at Farnham.

So, while Tiny slept, Wilfred was taking his solitary breakfast ; and the noise which awoke her, and for which she could not account, was made by the wheels of the dog-cart which carried him rapidly away over the fresh gravel-path under her bedroom window.

Wilfred Lane had passed a restless night. He

could not shut his eyes to the impropriety of Tiny's manner. It was a new development, for which he was totally unprepared. In the midst of what he had suffered about Captain Foy, he had been sustained by the belief, that when once Tiny recovered from her glamour all her affections would return to himself. He knew that she could neither mistake nor doubt his entire devotion to her. This pure and true love had utterly effaced the fevered and troubled passion of his youth, and Wilfred had not a thought apart from Tiny.

Her love was his very life. She had entwined herself so completely around his whole being, that the world was to him Tiny—and Tiny was the world.

He realized that their position was a difficult one ; a secret understanding must always be such ; and fearing that his presence hampered her, he resolved to leave the Castle without seeing her. One thing was obvious; it was high time Tiny should abstain of her own free will from actions which the commonest sense of right and wrong condemned. If she could flirt with the first man into whose society she was intimately thrown after her feeling for Foy subsided, Wilfred felt the love she professed to give him unworthy of his acceptance. His holding her to their mutual promise would only sooner or later bring about a calamity to both. At present there was time for Tiny ; no one knew of the tie between them.

When General Drummond told Miss Tiny Harewood, as she sat down to breakfast, of Wilfred's departure, that young lady was, for one moment, disconcerted ; but, seeing Mr. Macnaghten's eyes fixed upon her, with a presence of mind worthy of a better cause she carelessly observed that her cousin had told her on their way from church that he feared he should be forced to leave early the next morning.

Lady Isabella was just about to say she understood that Wilfred had only remembered these papers late on the preceding night, when something in Tiny's face arrested the words on her lips ; and, as Gertrude at that moment began to discuss a letter just received from Dublin, the conversation was fortunately turned into another channel.

As soon as Tiny got back to her own room, this strange little damsel gave vent to her disappointment; and, after crying for a good half hour, opened her writing-case, and, taking out a sheet of foreign letter paper, wrote as follows :

" Oh ! Wil, I am so thoroughly ashamed of myself; do forgive me this once for making you angry, and I will never do so again.   I am utterly miserable, and I think you have punished me very cruelly by going away without saying one word to me. ˙ I don't know how this state of things came about, and I look upon the whole affair as so curious that I don't understand myself in the least.   I frankly confess that I have given way to my old wicked spirit, and I know your confidence in me is completely shaken.

"But is it not better, Wil, for you to know me as I really am? You cannot help and guide me, if you do not. I think one of your highest points is your entire belief in those you love; but you never can be sufficient or good for a person, if you are blind to their faults. And the sort of life I am leading, away from you, is so bad for my disposition, that you ought to pity, rather than to blame me. You will find that I shall be quite different after June; and you don't know how intensely I long for the time when we shall be always together. Have patience till then, with this little girl you have made so miserable to-day. I would rather you should write me volumes of scoldings, than have thoughts of which you will not tell me. Believe me, Wil, as you love me, the hope of our future life together is the most precious thing in the world to me, for I feel my life fast clinging round yours. It would indeed be a terrible wrench to break it asunder now. So don't punish me any more for what has really been a foolish piece of nonsense, of which I am heartily ashamed. I don't know how it all came about; I suppose it was through this odious play, which I now hate and detest. Shall I throw it up? Write by return of post; for if you don't like me to act, I will give up my part at once. Oh, Wil, I am so wretched! I think I scarcely

11*

deserved such a severe punishment after all. I
shall not have a moment's peace till I hear you
have really forgiven

"Your penitent little

" TINY."

What could Wilfred say when he received this
letter? Poor infatuated fellow! He began to
agree with Tiny, and to think he need not have
left the Castle so hastily. The foolish nonsense
between Tiny and Macnaghten had by no means
deserved such a severe measure. After all, it was
that noisy young man who was really to blame—
it was his conduct which had drawn every one's attention to Tiny; and Wilfred, instead of letting
his wrath fall on the right object, had deprived
himself of the day in the country to which he had
looked forward with such pleasure, and made his
poor little Tiny wretched as well.

He was clearly a stupid blundering idiot, and
unable to fathom the mysterious depths of a
woman's delicate nature!

He sat down and wrote to Tiny, and begged her
not to give up the play. He confessed he had
left, because his private relationship with her
made it impossible for him either to witness or
prevent the attentions another man chose to pay
her. He thought she had been wrong to allow
Macnaghten to assume such a footing with her;
but he could not doubt her real fidelity to himself

after the letter he had just received. " At the same time," he added, " it seems to me, Tiny, that, lacking as we do the public acknowledgments and safeguards which such ties as ours generally receive in the world, we are doubly bound to cherish our private position, and to remember the duties we owe to each other."

Before Tiny received this answer, she was evidently anxious and depressed ; and discomfited the young Guardsman not a little by the snubs she administered whenever he attempted to resume the old familiarities she had allowed before her cousin's visit. Once assured of Wilfred's forgiveness, Tiny soon recovered her spirits, and, with them, her dislike of appearing disagreeable to any one ; and, as it was obviously disagreeable to Mr. Reginald Macnaghten to be checked in his advances, Tiny soon permitted them as freely as before.

The play went off gloriously ; and on the afternoon of the second performance Lady Harewood and her two daughters arrived.

Tiny acted her part to perfection, for, in truth, the character of *Helen* in Sheridan Knowles' ." Hunchback " exactly suited her.

Her sisters, who were in total ignorance of the flirtation with Reginald Macnaghten, noticed the peculiar look exchanged between them on the stage, when the latter, as *Modus*, exclaims:

"Your hand upon it ! "

And Tiny answers:

> " Hand and heart.
> Hie to thy dressing-room, and I'll to mine.
> Attire thee for the altar—so will I,
> Whoe'er may claim me, thou'rt the man shall have me."

Encouraged by that glance, and Tiny's excited manner, Reginald induced her, later in the evening, to throw an opera cloak over her shoulders, and to come on to the terrace, away from the crowded and heated rooms.

The night was cold and clear, for the moon was at the full, and every little blade of grass could be seen as plainly as at noonday. They walked slowly to the end of the terrace, and then Reginald insisted on sitting down for one moment in the summer-house, which commanded a fine view of the exquisite landscape before them. Everything looked so lovely and mysterious in the moonlight, that Tiny's senses were quite bewitched.

There was something in Reginald's manner which told her that it was impossible to escape the inevitable explanation. " Under all the circumstances," thought Tiny, " would it not be better to have it over at once ? "

She had not long to wait before he told her how he loved her, and entreated her to be his wife ; and without waiting for any answer, the impetuous young man put his arms round her and kissed her passionately.

"Stay, Mr. Macnaghten," cried Tiny, disengaging herself as best she could; "you have quite mistaken me. I thought you understood me better than to do this. I have often said enough to make you know that we could never be anything but friends; and if you do not control yourself, I shall feel very angry. It is unmanly of you," she continued, hastily springing up from her seat, and getting out of the summer-house on to the terrace, where the moonlight seemed to offer her some protection, "to abuse my confidence by such conduct. I feel very angry with you, indeed I do."

If Tiny had said "very frightened of you" it would have better expressed her meaning, for Reginald's violence had positively alarmed her.

He had felt so sure of a different answer, and was so excited by the acting and various glasses of champagne imbibed between the scenes, that Tiny's rebuff fairly staggered him. The way in which she had acted the part of *Helen* was so real and lifelike, that he had allowed himself to be carried away by the notion that, if an engagement existed (of which he had some dim surmise) between herself and that grave cousin, Tiny was ready to throw it over for his sake, and meant him to understand this, when she exclaimed with so much significance—

"Whoe'er may claim me, thou'rt the man shall have me."

Stammering out an apology, Reginald declared

he was so excited, he was more like a madman than anything else that night.

"Well then," said Tiny, feeling more secure as they neared the little side door, through which they had made their exit from the ball-room, "let us consider that your temporary fit of insanity is over, and do not let this subject ever be resumed."

He was on the point of speaking, when Tiny stopped him by saying, in a gentler voice, "I am sorry to pain you. You cannot think how it hurts me;" for she saw the young man was growing deadly pale. "It has been a great mistake. I am already engaged to my cousin, but you must not speak of it."

Reginald Macnaghten was silent. Tiny's words and manner told him he had nothing to hope, and he was struggling with his disappointment, which was real; for he had learnt to love this girl who had only trifled with him.

"Come, Reginald," said Tiny, calling him for the first time by his Christian name, "*give me your hand on it*, and let us be friends. I like you very much," she said, holding out her hand, "and should care to have you for a friend."

He kissed it, for he could not speak; but, instead of following her into the house, allowed her to pass in alone, and without another word, walked rapidly from the terrace into the dark shrubbery beyond.

That night Reginald Macnaghten never reappeared in the ball-room ; some hours later he was found in his room ; having retired, he said, with a violent headache.

Now that Tiny realized what she had done, she was sorry for it ; but, unfortunately, her repentance came too late ; and, in this instance, was accompanied by so many fears on her own account, that she had enough to do to think of how she should get out of this business with the least blame to herself.

It was a great relief to think that she was going away the next morning, or rather that very day ; for the sun had risen long before her sisters left her in undisturbed possession of her room, and with thoughts which were anything but calm and pleasant.

" At any rate," said Tiny to herself, " it was fortunate that Wilfred could not get leave of absence ; and yet, perhaps, if he had come down to the play, this last catastrophe might have been avoided."

She felt she should never dare confess all to him, for she knew she had acted foolishly in going out on the terrace ; her own sense told her that, in doing so, she provoked the declaration which followed ; and when she recalled the pained expression of Reginald's face as she last saw it, before he strode away into the shrubbery to conceal his emotion, a genuine regret came over her, and a sense of shame for having indulged her vanity at his expense.

But Tiny hated to think of what pained her, and consoled herself with a sweeping condemnation of her mother, for forcing her to conceal her position with Wilfred—of Wilfred, for not being present to take care of her—and of Reginald Macnaghten, for not restraining his feelings—and then she fell into a peaceful sleep, as if nothing whatever had happened, and she had never given a human being a moment's disquietude

CHAPTER XXXII.

"O purblind race of miserable men,
How many among us at this very hour
Do forge a life-long trouble for ourselves,
By taking true for false, and false for true."
Idylls of the King.

FOR the next few weeks Tiny astonished everybody by her eagerness to go to all the balls and parties for which the Harewoods received cards.

When alone with Wilfred she was constrained and nervous. She had not told him about Reginald Macnaghten's proposal, and was in constant dread of his hearing more about her conduct at Bellingham Castle than he knew already. If *that* displeased him, Tiny wondered what he would say if he knew *all* which had taken place since she wrote that penitent letter. The whole thing made her so restless and unhappy, that she craved for fresh excitement, and was never satisfied without it.

Nor was Wilfred happy. He could not disengage his affections from this enticing little piece of naughtiness, and yet his illusion was gone—gone far more completely than he thought it even that miserable night when he paced up and down the deck of the yacht at Ryde, and for the first time learned that Tiny loved another when she promised to be his wife.

And so these two, who, a few weeks before, had seemed so bound up in each other that nothing could sever them, began to grow wider and wider apart, until they were once more united by a common sorrow.

During this time, Wilfred Lane devoted himself more than ever to his work. His daily visit to Grosvenor Crescent was no longer expected as a matter of course. If he came, he found the drawing-room so full that he had no chance of a quiet talk with Tiny; if he dined there, she often left before dessert to prepare for some ball, to which she had promised to accompany Lady Harewood; and their quiet Sunday afternoons were now constantly broken into by interruptions which Wilfred knew well enough Tiny would have evaded in earlier days.

Still, he clung obstinately to the belief that all this sprang from the unnatural state of things to which Lady Harewood forced their submission. He thought that Tiny's restless love of excitement would subside, and the happiness she had expressed in her old letters from Rome would be hers, when she was settled in a quiet little home of her own, for which he so impatiently sighed. Tiny, too, often spoke of her happiness as certain, when removed from an atmosphere which, she assured Wilfred, she loathed and detested.

Such was the state of things on the 31st of May, between these two who had once thought it impossible to wait till then for the marriage which was to make them as publicly one, as their hearts long since had made them.

Wilfred was on his way to speak to Lady Harewood that evening, when he met one of his aunt's servants, who gave him a note from Tiny, begging him by no means to come to the house, because Madeline, who had been very poorly for the last few days, had scarlet fever, and the whole household was in confusion.

He had no fears for himself, having had the scarlet fever at Harrow; but, knowing he might convey the infection to others, he felt he must refrain from going to Tiny; for what would Lady Slade say, if she heard that Mr. Lane attended the War Office as usual, after visiting Grosvenor Crescent under present circumstances? With an expression which did not sound like a blessing on the rising generation of little Slades, he retraced his steps in the direction of his own chambers.

During the next few days constant notes passed between them, for Wilfred was not only anxious about Madeline, but in hourly dread lest Tiny should take the fever.

At first the accounts were favorable; but, by the end of the week, bad symptoms appeared;

and the doctors warned them all to prepare for the worst. After a night of great suspense, Wilfred received a line from Tiny, to say that poor Madeline had sunk from exhaustion at four o'clock that bright June morning; and Lady Harewood was so much alarmed lest any fresh case should break out, that she had resolved to leave the infected house that very day, and had actually despatched Watson to engage rooms at Walmer, as the quietest place they could think of in their distress.

Poor Tiny's letter was blotted all over with tears, for she was heart-broken at the sudden loss of her favorite sister, and horrified at the idea of leaving the house as soon as ever Madeline ceased to breathe.

Of course, Wilfred was thankful to hear of this plan, as it was evident the fever was of a malignant kind; but he felt very deeply the death of a cousin with whom so many early associations were connected.

How differently this first week in June passed to what any of them had expected!

Every day brought Wilfred a letter from Walmer, which he eagerly opened, fearing it might contain news of further illness; but the cruel fever had done its work: gradually all alarm subsided; and, at the end of three weeks, Sir Thomas Slade (unknown to his wife) told Mr. Lane he might safely run down and see poor Lady Harewood and his cousins.

On the following Saturday afternoon, Wilfred astonished his aunt and cousins by walking into the small house they occupied, facing the sea.

When Tiny saw him her grief burst out afresh, for they had not met since Madeline's death ; and directly they were alone, she hid her face on his shoulder, and, refusing to be comforted, wept as if her very heart would break.

After dinner they walked together on the beach ; but although they both shrank from speaking of their hope of future happiness, in the presence of this new sorrow, they seemed to be nearer to each other ; nearer than they had been for many weeks.

The next morning Wilfred took Tiny across the fields to the church at Upper Deal. On their return, Lady Harewood consulted them about a very kind letter she had received from Lady Lothian, inviting them all to her place in Scotland. A few years before, Lady Lothian had lost her own daughter in scarlet fever ; and she begged the Harewoods to come to her as soon as they felt inclined, promising that no one should intrude on them, for she knew how to sympathize with their deep sorrow.

Wilfred had never seen Lady Lothian, as the Harewoods had made her acquaintance in Rome ; but he was much pleased with her letter, and, when they talked it over, he advised her offer should be accepted. It was accordingly settled that they should propose to be with her the second week in July ; and as it was considered more prudent to avoid Grosvenor Crescent altogether, Wilfred was to engage rooms at the Euston Square Hotel, to enable them to rest one night in London, and to take the day mail to Edinburgh.

Tiny wrote every day, whilst she was at the sea-side—letters full of the old love—and again told Wilfred how she longed for the time which would put an end to a separation which became more and more wearisome.

On the fourteenth of July the Harewoods left Walmer for the Euston Square Hotel, where Wilfred was waiting to receive them.

He took the first possible opportunity of telling Lady Harewood that, although this sorrow had prevented their claiming her promise on the first of June, they trusted she would consent to their marriage during the autumn, and added he was about to see a cottage at Chislehurst, to which Tiny had taken a fancy.

Lady Harewood seemed considerably softened by her recent grief, and said she had been expecting this communication, and would talk to Tiny when they were at Lady Lothian's ; she also requested him to write fully about ways and means after his visit to Chislehurst. Then she wished him good-by, rather more cordially than usual, and retired with Charlotte in order to give Wilfred a quiet half hour with Tiny.

Before they parted that night, Tiny unburdened her heart, and confessed the extent of Reginald Macnaghten's influence over her. She spoke, too, again of Captain Foy; of her unrest and craving for excitement; and then assured Wilfred of her perfect love for himself, and her happiness in looking forward to the day which should unite them forever.

Still, as Wilfred Lane walked home, he determined to give her the chance of once more reconsidering the whole matter, but resolved to wait until she had settled down at Dunoon. In the meantime he went to Chislehurst, and made every inquiry, as if the result were certain to be in accordance with his wishes. Tiny soon sent him news of their arrival in Edinburgh, and their subsequent welcome from Lady Lothian at her lovely place on the banks of the Loch Lomond.

CHAPTER XXXIII.

" His grand excellence was this, that he was genuine."
THOMAS CARLYLE.

WHEN Tiny had been about ten days in Scotland she received the following letter :

" MY OWN DARLING TINY,

" I have been thinking so much of all you told me the night before you left London, that I feel I ought to ask you to reconsider your position with regard to me. This separation has been brought about in such a strange and mysterious manner, that it almost seems as if it had been sent on purpose to enable you once more to deliberate before your final decision. So now, Tiny, believe me, when I say I honestly want you to consider yourself unfettered by any previous promise; as having, in fact, your choice to make. Do not suppose, my beloved, that I write thus because I love you less, or am a shade less eager for our marriage ; on the contrary, Tiny, I seem every day to love and need you more ; but I love you so infinitely more than I do my own happiness, that I can surrender it to yours. Do not fear to trust me.

If there is any doubt on your mind; if you have the shadow of a suspicion that life with me will not give you all you can imagine possible under such circumstances, I think you are bound to hesitate, even now, at the eleventh hour, in spite of any present suffering and humiliation to me. You see, my darling, one point has been made clear to you this year, and your doubts and difficulties respecting Captain Foy are forever set at rest. This gives you a far better opportunity of deciding your own future, than could be the case while your little mind was harassed by all these cruel perplexities which tormented it so long. But, Tiny, I sometimes tremble lest you should have mistaken your feeling for me, because I was able in the first instance unconsciously to help you to bear your sorrow, and, after you confided in me, to sympathize with every little difficulty and pain it brought you. Therefore, I want you once more to consider the whole matter. Do not, for any fear of bringing trouble upon me, hesitate to do what is best for your own happiness. Remember, my darling, you would bring a far greater misery upon me in the end, if I found, a few weeks after our marriage, that it did not yield you all the joy you expected. Tiny, the thought that I could never help you, never release you from such a bondage, would be intolerable to me. For both our sakes I implore you to make no mistake about your love for me.

12

"Let me speak plainly to you, which I can do much more calmly than when present with you.

"It is not that I love you less, or that I can—even while I tell you to choose afresh—think of parting with you without a thorough upset of my life and the only happiness I have ever pictured—the future I have treasured for years! But I dare not (after what I saw at Bellingham, and what you have since told me about your feeling for Macnaghten) refrain from offering to set you free from the tie which has hitherto bound us.

"It is easier, Tiny, to say things than to forget them; just as it was easier for me to be angry at Bellingham, rather than wise and patient; but what you said and did then, took away from me the confidence I had in our future, and left in its place a thousand doubts and difficulties.

"When I first told you I loved you, and asked you to be my wife, you made me believe that your love for me was so completely a part of your nature, that nothing short of our marriage would satisfy you: and that the happiness of such a union would more than counterbalance any trials and drawbacks incidental to our position. If I had ever doubted this, I should have felt it wrong to offer your mother the decided opposition I did. When I learnt for the first time at Ryde the existence of a previous attachment, you know, Tiny, what I wished to do. I allowed you to overrule me, because I believed events would turn out as

they have, in one way ; but I never dreamt that
any other feeling would take the slightest hold
upon you—even to the extent it did at Bellingham.

" I cannot write calmly, after all ; and I don't
know that many words are wanted. All I have
to say is, that I implore you, my darling, to
be very sure you are making no mistake now.
Unless you love me wholly our marriage will simply expose you to a thousand miseries and dangers, of which you have at present no conception.
Without love, Tiny—the deepest love of your
whole being—it will be destitute of the greatest
safeguard against temptations to which some
natures are peculiarly liable. Think over this
while you are away from me, my darling ; you
are better able now to come to a clear decision
about the state of your own mind, and what will
best promote your future welfare. Do not hesitate to choose what seems happiest for you, because your kind little heart shrinks from wounding
me ; remember I am a great strong fellow, and
can better face this trouble, than you could cope
with such a life-long difficulty as an incomplete
marriage.

" I know too much of the wretchedness and sin
such marriages produce, ever to forget it ; and
therefore solemnly conjure you, Tiny, not to link
your fate with mine if you have one doubt about
your affection for me. The thought that I might

prove your evil, and not your good, has sent me
down on my knees more than once, and I would
welcome any present desolation for myself rather
than run such a fearful risk for you, my own dear
one—dearer far than my own soul.

" Yours,

" WILFRED LANE."

" DUNOON.

" I would not answer your letter, my darling
Wil, in a hurry; so I kept it for two days in my
pocket, and have read it through a great many
times since it came.

" You are a dear, noble, generous-hearted fellow; but there was no occasion for you to write
as you did, or to place so much weight upon what
I have said and done, when I was in an ill-conditioned state.

If I wanted anything to convince me that I
never could be happy without you, this separation
would have done it.   I feel such a blank, and one
does not quite know why it is, till I picture what
this place would be like if you were only here;
and then I find it is your absence which makes the
want.   My own Wil ! our life together is the only
one I can think of with any satisfaction ; and I
feel sure it will be a happy one, if, as you said in
our last sweet talk together, we make up our
minds to do all we can for each other's happiness.
Certainly, it is only by doing my duty by you

that I shall ever get any real happiness, or do myself any good; you must think the same, and then
our little home will be a sweet and peaceful one.
I do indeed realize this, and am ready to do my
best. I think I must succeed better than I have
before, because all seems so much clearer. You
may be sure that it is no sudden impulse which
makes me say this. I may be changeable in temperament; but I am certain that my feeling for
you is based upon the deepest part of my mind,
and life would be incomplete without you.

" I quite understand your letter, Wilfred, and
feel for you in a way which will, I hope, make me
in the future more considerate to you than I have
been in the past. I know I was very wrong about
Reginald Macnaghten, or rather, I missed the
highest right, chiefly from not seeing what I was
doing; and, as I am quite, *quite* certain that a life
with you would secure for me a far greater amount
of happiness than anything else in the world, I will
be more unselfish in the future. I am writing this
after some very serious thought, Wil.

"Believe me, I could not part with you, any
better than you could part with me. The happiest moment in the day is when I come down
and find a letter from you on the breakfast-table;
and the next best—when I sit down to answer it.
Every day makes me more dependent upon you;
no, my darling, I never could do without you
now; and you would be more than satisfied if you

knew how I am longing for the time when we shall
always be together in a peaceful little home of our
own.   I was counting even yesterday the days to
that dearest event, and wondering if mamma
would insist on our waiting until the six dreariest
months I have ever spent in my life are completed.   So good-by, my own ; for my own you
always, *always* must be, and that is your answer.
I kiss your dear ring as I write.   I have no time
for more.

" Your own little
" TINY."

This letter extinguished Wilfred's last lingering
suspicion ; his whole nature rejoiced in the thought
of his darling's love ; and he thanked God for this
rich gift, and prayed to be able to make her
happy.

He pursued the owner of the cottage at Chislehurst with renewed vigor, and at last obtained his
definite answer.   Mr. Hall was about to leave
England, and wished to sell his cottage, together
with the old oak furniture and the curious cabinets
it contained.   The house was fitted up with such
perfect taste, that Tiny used often to say if she
herself had planned it, she could not have succeeded better.

After a few days' negotiation, matters were
finally arranged ; and, in spite of the heavy sum it
required, Wilfred succeeded in obtaining the cot-

tage, as Mr. Hall agreed to give him immediate possession, and to let part of the purchase-money stand over for another year. So, when the night mail travelled down to Scotland on the following Monday, it carried a letter which much delighted the little person to whom it was addressed.

" MY DARLING TINY,

" Your letter has made me the happiest man in the whole world ! I will never again have another doubt about your love, so I shall 'let the dead past bury its dead,' including Mr. Reginald Macnaghten, and, by way of acting in the 'living present,' as the poet says, I have just signed, sealed, and paid over the greater part of the purchase-money for that queer little place at Chislehurst, which took your fancy so last year. As Mr. Hall is going to live in Florence, he wished to sell the whole house as it stands ; so you may now consider yourself the mistress of this quaint little cottage. How I wish you could put yourself into an envelope, and come back in the next post-bag, to preside over your new possession and me ! I am getting so hungry for you, Tiny, that, when I do get hold of you, I shall devour you altogether —there will be nothing of you left. I shall be like the old bear in the story, 'who growled over her a little while and then ate her up.' Well, if we had not waited all this time, I should never have saved enough money, so it is all right, I suppose.

But we shall not want to buy any more houses, so please tell your mother we really cannot wait any longer. I don't see at all why she should not agree to our being married in September, without any fuss or ceremony. It will then be two years since that day when you found out what those little marks meant in my Browning. Well, my own, if I felt so for you then, I do ten thousand times more now. You seem a very part of me—and the best part, too. And, after that sweet letter you have written in answer to my offer to let you spread your little wings and fly away, I feel as I used to do when I was a schoolboy at Harrow, the day before the holidays. If I don't take care I shall be playing off a practical joke upon Sir Thomas Slade !

" So you were kissing my ring for want of something better, eh ? Ah, my little sunshine, if I could only gather you up in my arms at this moment ! Well—Christmas Day will, I hope, find us sitting by our own fireside at Chislehurst. The very thought of it makes me feel like a giant ! God bless you.

" Yours forever,

" W. L."

This news made Tiny wild with joy. She had taken such a fancy to this cottage, that she declared she would rather live there than in any other place in England; and, for the next fortnight, she was continually suggesting a hundred little alterations she wanted made in their future home; and told Wilfred, above everything, to " cultivate earwigs, as no place was really delightful without them."

Lady Harewood was interested in hearing about the house and their future plans, but still said she would not allow the marriage to take place before the end of the prescribed six months.

" So," wrote Tiny, " it must be November instead of June."

12*

CHAPTER XXXIV.

*" I would not have that exotic virtue which is kept from the
chill blast, hidden from evil, without any permission to be exposed
to temptation. That alone is virtue which has good placed before
it and evil, and, seeing the evil, chooses the good."*

REV. FREDERIC ROBERTSON.

ONE lovely morning towards the end of August,
Lady Lothian and her guests stepped through an
open window on to the lawn at Dunoon, while
discussing the contents of the letter-bag, which had
arrived during breakfast.

Lady Lothian had been surprised by a letter
from her son, who had reached London from St.
Petersburgh nearly a fortnight before he was expected. He wanted to bring a friend down for
some grouse shooting; and Lady Lothian was
extremely uncomfortable, because she fancied that
any society would at present be distasteful to
Lady Harewood.

On reading this letter, Lady Lothian had expressed her astonishment at her son's return, and
she felt it was useless to delay mooting the other
point to which it referred. " Herbert wishes to
come here next Saturday; and talks of bringing

his friend, Henry Talbot, with him. Will you tell
me frankly, dear Lady Harewood, if this would be
disagreeable to you and the girls? If you feel it
an intrusion, Herbert can easily go to his own
moor in Aberdeenshire, without coming here at
all."

" I would not, on any account, keep Lord
Lothian away," replied her guest. " The very
thought of such a thing makes me uncomfortable
at trespassing so long on your hospitality ; and we
really ought to be going home."

" I will not hear of that. You promised me to
stay until the end of September, and by that time
I do hope to see you looking a little stronger.
Poor Tiny, too, is only just beginning to get a little color on her cheeks."

" Oh, I am very well," said Tiny, slipping her
hand into Lady Lothian's, with whom she was a
special favorite, for she often reminded her of the
daughter she had lost. For her sake and Charlotte's, Lady Lothian was glad that her son talked
of coming with his friend; for though the young
men would spend the greater part of the day on
the moors, the very fact of their being in the
house would add to its general liveliness.

There is a certain amount of decorum which
ought to be observed ; but when grief is genuine,
people need not be afraid of making their outward circumstances as cheerful as possible.

And certainly the arrival of Lord Lothian and

Mr. Talbot made a difference to everybody in the house, although at first the days were spent in the pursuit of grouse; and when they returned, tired with their sport, they did not always join the ladies after dinner.

But, before very long, an excursion was planned to Loch Katrine and the Trossachs, and sundry boating expeditions followed. Tiny's letters to Wilfred were filled with descriptions of the lovely scenery through which they passed; and he rejoiced to find how rapidly she was recovering her spirits, and that the seclusion Lady Harewood at first rigidly enforced had come to so timely an end.

But when Tiny's letters became shorter than before, he almost grudged the time spent in these mountain and boating excursions; and, at last, when a whole week passed and he never heard at all, he felt anxious, and despatched a grumbling epistle to Dunoon.

Tiny answered by saying " the days were so full, that even letters to him ' seemed a push ; ' "—an expression which somewhat astonished him, though he did not wonder at her raptures over " an atmosphere which seemed to have so little of the nineteenth century about it." " I cannot describe the feeling," she said; "but there is such an absence of that irritating shallowness of perpetual *go*, which means nothing, and produces nothing lasting, and never can do any one any good."

In the same letter she said :

" I read Thomas-à-Kempis every day, as you asked me to do. The thing he appears to dwell on most is the necessity of training the mind to the inward, and not to the outward condition of life. That is, as you often say, my greatest difficulty ; and habit has increased my natural tendency to externals. But, Wil, I can honestly say that I derive very little pleasure from them ; at least, the pleasure which comes is so unsatisfactory that it is nearer like vexation. I read such a glorious chapter in Proverbs this morning ; one verse in it made me think for a long time : it was about the spirit of a man being the candle of the Lord reaching the inmost parts ; that spirit, I find, is the only finger-post to the path where one's duty lies, and I try to test my feeling for you by that, and to act accordingly. I quite understand your complaining about my letters. I don't know why I feel so disinclined to write about our proceedings ; but you don't know the people here, and details of going out and coming in are only interesting when connected with people you know something of."

This last sentence seemed to Wilfred strangely inconsistent with Tiny's previous delight in telling him every passing incident of her daily life.

CHAPTER XXXV.

"Till from the straw the flail the corn doth beat
Until the chaff be purgèd from the wheat,
Yea, till the mill the grains in pieces tear
The richness of the flour will scarce appear.
So, till men's persons great afflictions touch.
If worth be found, their worth is not so much,
Because, like wheat in straw, they have not yet
That value which in threshing they may get.
For, till the bruising flail of God's corrections
Have threshèd out of us our vain affections;
Till those corruptions which do misbecome us
Are by thy sacred Spirit winnowed from us;
Until from us the straw of worldly treasures,
Till all the dusty chaff of empty pleasures,
Yea! till His flail upon us He doth lay
To thresh the husk of this our flesh away
And leave the soul uncovered; nay, yet more,
Till God shall make our very spirit poor,
We shall not up to highest wealth aspire,
But then we shall; and that is my desire."

WITHER.

SEPTEMBER passed away, and the first week in October found the Harewoods still at Dunoon. For ten days Wilfred had not heard from Tiny: one morning, however, he found a thick envelope on the breakfast-table; eagerly seizing it, and pushing aside his breakfast, he sat down to devour its contents.

It commenced with an account of two days spent in Arran, and then continued, after a break:

" This autumn weather, the falling leaves, and the lovely tints, have such a strange effect upon me. Such a view we saw yesterday as we were walking home—thick mists rose in the valley, which were bright pink where the sun shone through them—deep blue where they were in shade—and the woods a thousand colors; cherry, orange, and every conceivable shade. The outlines were as magical as Turner's, or some of Gustave Doré's drawings."

Here the letter broke off, and was, apparently, continued a few days later:

" Oh, Wil, life is very difficult, with all its complicated feelings and necessities! But I suppose we are given something inside us to guide us in these complications. We stumble, fall, and dissemble; and the dissembling returns upon ourselves. The heart alone knoweth its own bitterness, but also alone knoweth its own comfort. Wilfred, the more I see of myself the more diffident I get about myself. Such a curious feeling has come into my life that I dare no longer deceive you. I have a feeling for Lord Lothian.

Dishonest I have not been, because I have deceived myself more than you. I came to you full of the intensest feeling towards another. Your superiority to me, in so many ways, gave me such a respect for you that it blinded me to the sin I was committing—and so it has been all along. The great good and strength you were to me, deadened the feeling that I was not all I should have been to you ; and my real affection—a thousand times greater now than when you first told me that you loved me—made me shrink from not trying to be all you wished me to be to you. This is the truth, Wil. You may well say that I ought to have said so when you wrote to me that letter some weeks ago, and asked me to think seriously of our life. I did think, to the best of my power, Wil darling ; and it then seemed to me that a life with you would be the best and happiest I could imagine.

" I thought that episode at Bellingham Castle was entirely my own fault, arising from self-indulgence and love of admiration. So it was ; and if this feeling were like it, I should consider it as unworthy as I consider that.

" God knows my strongest desire now is that you may not suffer from my being what I am if I can help it. Though you would be wrong to think I am happy, yet, when Lord Lothian asked me for my love, I felt if I refused it him I should be shutting out of my life the brightest glow of happiness I have ever imagined since that miserable affair with Captain Foy.

" Since that winter at Windsor, I have not even imagined any happiness in life till this time—I mean happiness which God puts into your nature without your asking for it or seeking it in any way. I know that happiness is not the goal of life, nor is it to be got by seeking it irrespectively of duty; and, Wil, believe me when I say I have tried to do what I ought to do in this matter.

" Throughout all my weaknesses and changes there is but one thing I am able steadily to believe and think of—the strength and help you have been to me. Wilfred, the growth of the little that is worth having in me, is solely connected with the time I have been so much with you. If the thought of me gives you pain, I would, if I could, obliterate myself from your memory; though I can hardly tell you what that would be to me. Whatever you may say or do, I shall never be able to be anything but your own Tiny; own in the best sense of the word—for the only part I respect in myself is closely united with something in you.

" Pity me, Wil, for I cannot be happy, knowing the wrong I have done to you.

"TINY."

When Wilfred finished reading this letter, he began it again, and read it through from begin-

ning to end. He did not seem able to understand it. At last his eyes fixed upon the words,
"I HAVE A FEELING FOR LORD LO-
THIAN." He repeated them aloud; and then
seemed so startled by the sound of his own voice,
that he sat looking at that sentence without attempting to move.

He was disturbed by the entrance of the servant
who came in to remove the breakfast, wondering
why Mr. Lane lingered such a long time over it;
wondering still more when she saw he had not
touched it. Before she could speak, Wilfred
thrust his letter into his breast-pocket, and, taking
up his hat, went down the stairs at once to avoid
observation.

The blow had so crushed him that he wandered
about the streets like a man in a dream. He was
neither conscious of where he walked, nor of the
crowd around him. Mechanically he took his
usual route to the War Office, but passed it without knowing he did so. He turned to the left, up
Regent Street, passed the Langham Hotel, on
through Portland Place, the Regent's Park—on,
on, to Primrose Hill, with his eyes on the ground,
and his lips every now and then murmuring,
"Tiny, Tiny!"

At last he suddenly remembered that it was
Saturday morning. There was some special work
to be done that day at the War Office; and after
this he had arranged to go to Chislehurst, for he

wanted the place to be in perfect order before Tiny returned. Oh, how he loathed the very name of Chislehurst now! It seemed to stab him in every vulnerable part, and brought ten thousand pangs in place of the happy confidence which had been his at this very hour yesterday. He hastily retraced his steps, and calling a Hansom cab, told the driver to hurry on to the War Office; and, as he walked up the steps, he involuntarily exclaimed, " God help the man she now says she loves ! "

When Mr. Lane apologized to Sir Thomas Slade for his late arrival, there was but little need to say he was ill; his face told the tale plainly enough. A headache, however, did duty for the real pain he was suffering; and after vainly attempting to work, Wilfred was forced to return home.

He locked himself into his room. Feeling faint and chilly, he poured out a tumbler of brandy and water, and drank it off; then putting a match to his fire, threw himself into the arm-chair before it, and sat hour after hour vacantly staring at the flickering blaze—perfectly stunned by this unexpected blow.

At last he drew out Tiny's letter; yes, there were the words—" *I have a feeling for Lord Lothian.*" Wilfred could see nothing else on the whole sheet but those terrible words—" *I have a feeling for Lord Lothian.*" He staggered to the

writing-table, and, unlocking a drawer, took out
several bundles of letters.   Here was the packet
from Rome—these, tied up with a lock of fair hair,
were the letters from Berkshire.   Opening the
foreign ones, he read them through ; and, as he
laid them back in the drawer, he thought the nov-
elist was right when he said there are no better
satires than letters.

"Vows—love—promises—confidences and gratitude—how queer-
ly they read after a while !   There ought to be a law in Vanity Fair
ordering the destruction of every written document (except receipted
tradesmen's bills) after a certain and proper period.   The quacks
and misanthropes who advertise indelible ink should be made to
perish along with their wicked discoveries.   The best ink for Vanity Fair use would be one that faded utterly in a couple of days, and
left the paper clean and blank, so that you might write on it to
somebody else."

Sweet   and   bitter   thoughts   were   crowding
through Wilfred's mind, as he sat resting his head
on his hands against the table—memories of infinite tendernesses he had received from Tiny ; days
and hours which never could be forgotten ; love
which no future falseness could ever quite efface !
Recollections came, too, of the hot and fatal passion of his youth—his sin was finding him out
after many days !

Morning dawned, and Wilfred still sat battling
with his misery.   He took up a pen, and, drawing
closer to the table, he began to write :

"Your letter, Tiny, was such a shock to me,

that I could not answer it as you requested, by return of post. I feel bewildered. It is scarcely three weeks since I received that dear and loving letter which I prized and believed in so—and now! What am I to think? what am I to say? When did you deceive yourself—then or now? There is but one conclusion, Tiny—you are utterly unstable; and I am powerless to save you, because the feeling of love and honor which you ought to have is wanting.

" After hours of battling with my own feelings, I can only pray that you may not live out your present fancy as you have your love for me. If you will indulge your perilous love of power, it must end in corrupting the high and glorious spirit which God meant to be the best part of you; but which you are extinguishing by this perpetual crucifixion of your higher nature.

" I do not want to blame you, Tiny; I know our position has been a very difficult one; with every one seeking to undermine our tie instead of strengthening it, none but a very firm true heart could have stood the test. But when you returned from Rome—but that was before you had lived through your feeling for me.

"Tiny, it is useless to write, and I am too bewildered to think—the misery of the last twenty-four hours seems simply unreal; you, another person. To think of life with you out of it, almost drives me mad; my mind seems to have lost its balance, and my very body seems shaken already by the blow. You ask me to help you. Tiny, I want help myself. The thought that you have any pain from which I cannot shield you, tortures me. You cannot be happy, my poor child, though you have not the misery I have to bear. Oh! Tiny, my own—I cannot write. No words can recall the past: all we have now to do is to bury it reverently, without recriminations—and may God help us both in our different kinds of need and misery! Tiny, though you have sinned in the past, I implore you to be good and true in your next relationship—for this I will never cease to pray.

" As for me, I have deserved this bitterness—you are simply the instrument of a just retribution ; nothing short of having my own happiness torn up by the very roots would ever have punished me as I deserve."

.   .   .   .   .

Just as Wilfred Lane finished writing, the Sunday-morning church-bells rang out as usual ; when he heard them, he gave a cry of pain, and, kneeling down, hid his face in his hands. The bitter sobs which broke from him for hours after told that the iron had entered his soul as only the hand of Tiny could have driven it.

FINIS.